BUDGETING 101

USING

AI

A beginner-friendly money guide for students and anyone starting from zero — with AI as your personal budgeting coach.

Written by

ERIC LEBOUTHILLIER

AcraSolution | 2025 1st Edition
www.acrasolution.com

Preface

Who this book is for

This book is for students, young adults, and anyone who feels lost when it comes to money. If you have zero experience with budgeting, saving, or planning, this guide was made for you. No big words, no confusing math — just the basics explained in plain language, step by step.

What to expect from this book

Inside, you'll learn how to track your money, spend smarter, and start saving — even if it's just a few dollars. You'll discover easy rules to follow, how to set goals, and how AI tools can help make everything simpler. By the end, you'll understand how to make a budget you can actually stick to, giving you more control, less stress, and a clear path toward your future.

LEGAL DISCLAIMER

This publication is intended solely for informational and educational purposes. It does not constitute legal, financial, medical, or professional advice. The content is not a substitute for consultation with qualified experts or licensed professionals in the relevant fields.

Portions of this work have been created or assisted by artificial intelligence (AI) tools. While every reasonable effort has been made to review, fact-check, and edit the content for clarity and accuracy, AI-generated information may occasionally contain errors, omissions, or generalized statements. The author and publisher do not guarantee the accuracy, completeness, or reliability of the information provided.

Readers are strongly encouraged to seek independent advice tailored to their personal circumstances from qualified legal, financial, healthcare, or compliance professionals before making decisions or taking action based on this content.

References to specific products, services, companies, websites, or technologies do not imply endorsement or affiliation unless explicitly stated. All trademarks and brand names mentioned remain the property of their respective owners.

The author and publisher disclaim any liability, loss, or risk incurred directly or indirectly from the use or misuse of this publication. This includes, but is not limited to, damages of any kind — including incidental, special, or consequential — arising out of the reliance on the material presented.

All references to laws, regulations, security standards, or industry guidelines are intended for general awareness only and may not reflect the most current legal developments. This publication is not intended to create, and receipt does not constitute, a client relationship with the author, publisher, or any affiliated entity.

By reading, accessing, or applying the content in this publication, you agree to do so at your own risk. If you do not accept these terms, you are advised to discontinue use of this material immediately.

Table of Contents

CHAPTER 1

What money in vs. money out means

What Money In vs. Money Out Means

You probably hear people talk about "managing money" or "budgeting," but let's start even simpler. Before you can manage money, you have to understand two basic things: **what comes in** and **what goes out.**

This is the foundation of everything else in your financial life. If you get this part wrong, everything else can fall apart.

What Does "Money In" Mean?

"Money in" is the money you receive. This is also called **income.**

Here are a few examples of **money in**:

- The paycheck from your part-time job
- Money your parents give you for allowance
- Birthday or holiday cash from friends or family
- Tips from a restaurant or delivery job
- A student grant or scholarship that includes spending money

If someone gives you money or if you earn it — it's *money in.*

Think of it like this:

Money in = What fills your wallet or bank account

You want to know **how much money you have coming in** each week or month, so you can plan what to do with it.

What Does "Money Out" Mean?

"Money out" is what you spend. This is also called **expenses**.

Here are some examples of **money out**:

- Buying snacks or lunch
- Paying for a Netflix subscription
- Buying clothes or shoes
- Filling up your gas tank
- Ordering food online
- Going out with friends
- Buying school supplies

If money leaves your pocket, wallet, or bank account — that's *money out*.

Think of it like this:

Money out = What drains your wallet or bank account

Why It Matters

Let's keep it simple. If you spend **more** than you bring in, you're going to run into problems.

Here's a basic formula:

If money in > money out = You're good.
If money out > money in = You're in trouble.

If you make $400 in a month and spend $420, you'll be short $20. That shortfall can lead to:

- Overdraft fees
- Credit card debt
- Borrowing money
- Feeling stressed or stuck

But if you make $400 and only spend $350, you have $50 left over — that's your **extra cushion**, also called savings.

Real-World Example: Meet Jayden

What happened:
Jayden is a college freshman. He works 15 hours a week at a coffee shop and makes about $500 per month. He uses the money for food, clothes, and going out with friends.

But Jayden never kept track of what was coming in or going out. At the end of every month, his bank account was nearly empty.

What went wrong:
Jayden thought he was spending "just a little here and there" — $10 on lunch, $25 on a shirt, $18 for a movie night. But it added up fast. One month, he overdrafted his account and got hit with a $35 fee — just because he didn't know how much he had left.

What we learn from it:
Even small expenses can build up if you're not paying attention. Without knowing your money in vs. money out, you can't make smart choices. Jayden started tracking both, and within two months, he had saved over $100 just by being more aware.

Tactical Best Practices

- **List all your money in:** Write down every source of income, even small ones.
- **Track your money out daily:** Use a free app or just write it in your phone notes.
- **Check your balance weekly:** Know what's left in your account before spending.
- **Notice patterns:** Do you always overspend on weekends? Food delivery? Track to find out.

Common Mistakes to Avoid

- Thinking small purchases don't matter — they do.
- Not knowing how much you actually earn or spend in a month.
- Ignoring your bank balance and assuming it's "probably fine."
- Only checking your money after it's already gone.

Checklist: Your First Step Toward Budgeting

- ✅ Write down how much money you earned this week/month
- ✅ List every time you spent money (even small stuff)
- ✅ Subtract your spending from your income
- ✅ See what's left — is it positive or negative?
- ✅ If it's negative, find out where to cut back

Conclusion

Understanding "money in vs. money out" is like learning to breathe before running a marathon. It's the most basic step, but the most important. If you don't know how much you're earning and how much you're spending, you'll always feel like money is slipping through your fingers.

But once you get this simple balance under control, everything else in budgeting becomes way easier.

Next Steps

Now that you understand what money in vs. money out means, you're ready to learn why **everyone** — even students — needs a budget. In the next section, we'll show you how budgeting isn't just for adults or people with "lots of money." It's for anyone who wants to feel more confident and in control.

Why Everyone Needs a Budget (Even Students)

When most people hear the word **"budget,"** they imagine something boring, complicated, or only for adults with full-time jobs. But here's the truth: if you have any money at all — even just $10 a week — you need a budget.

A budget isn't about saying *no* to everything. It's about knowing where your money goes and making sure it works **for you**, not against you.

What Is a Budget, Really?

Let's make it simple:

A **budget** is a **plan** for your money.

It's just a way to decide:

- How much money is coming in
- What you need to spend it on
- What you want to save for
- And how to avoid running out

It's not complicated. You don't need an accountant, fancy tools, or a finance degree.

You just need to **pay attention** and make choices on purpose — instead of by accident.

Why Students Need a Budget Too

Even if you're not paying rent or bills yet, managing money is still part of your life. In fact, **this is the perfect time** to start budgeting. Why?

Because the habits you build now will carry into adulthood. If you learn how to handle $100 wisely, you'll be ready to handle $1,000 or $10,000 later.

Here's why students — especially — benefit from having a budget:

1. Limited income means every dollar counts

Most students live on part-time income, allowance, or financial aid. That means your money isn't unlimited — so you have to make it stretch.

2. It's easy to overspend without noticing

Small purchases — coffee, snacks, subscriptions — add up quickly. Without a budget, you won't know where your money's going until it's already gone.

3. You can avoid debt early

Credit cards, overdrafts, or borrowing from friends can feel like an easy fix. But those choices can trap you in a cycle of stress and money problems. Budgeting helps you stay ahead of that.

4. You can start building savings, even small

Saving just $10 a week can add up fast. With a budget, you can see where that $10 can come from — and set it aside for something meaningful.

Real-World Example: Meet Karla

What happened:
Karla is a second-year college student. She gets $600 a month from a combination of part-time work and support from her parents. She used to spend freely — $8 here, $12 there — and never tracked it.

One month, her phone bill bounced. She had spent too much on food delivery and forgot the bill was due. Her phone got temporarily disconnected.

What went wrong:
Karla had no plan. She just "hoped" her money would last until the end of the month. But hope isn't a strategy. Without a budget, she had no idea what she could afford and what she couldn't.

What we learn from it:
A budget helps you **see problems before they happen**. After that incident, Karla started using a simple budget — writing down her fixed costs, planning her spending, and setting reminders. She hasn't missed a bill since, and even started saving $50 a month for travel.

What Happens When You Don't Budget?

If you don't control your money, your money will control you.

Here's what *not* budgeting can lead to:

- Always wondering where your money went
- Running out before the end of the month
- Borrowing or relying on credit
- Missing payments or bills
- Constant stress and second-guessing

Without a budget, you're guessing. With one, you're planning. That's a huge difference.

What Happens When You Do Budget?

Budgeting gives you:

- **Confidence** — you know what you can afford
- **Control** — you're not reacting, you're deciding
- **Clarity** — your money has a purpose
- **Freedom** — because once your needs are covered, you can enjoy the extras

Even if your income is small, a budget turns it into something powerful.

Tactical Best Practices for Student Budgeting

- **Use the 50/30/20 rule (starter version):**
  - 50% needs (food, phone, transport)
  - 30% wants (fun, hobbies, non-essentials)
  - 20% savings (even if small)
- **Set a weekly money check-in:** Pick one day a week to see how much you've spent and what's left.
- **Use cash for tricky categories:** If you overspend on snacks or coffee, withdraw a set amount in cash and don't spend more.
- **Use a free budgeting app or spreadsheet:** There are many simple, student-friendly tools available.

Common Mistakes to Avoid

- Thinking budgeting is only for "rich people" or "adults"
- Believing you'll just "figure it out" as you go
- Not tracking your spending because it "feels fine"
- Thinking budgeting is about saying no — it's actually about saying yes *on purpose*

Checklist: Start Your First Budget

- ☑ Write down your monthly income (jobs, allowance, etc.)
- ☑ List your regular monthly costs (phone, transportation, food)
- ☑ Estimate your flexible spending (like fun or takeout)
- ☑ Choose a small savings goal ($10/week, etc.)
- ☑ Check your numbers — does your income cover all of this?
- ☑ Adjust until your plan works — then stick to it

Conclusion

Budgeting isn't about being perfect or strict — it's about being **aware**. Even students with small incomes need to know where their money goes. If you start now, you'll avoid the stress and mistakes most people make later. Budgeting gives you freedom — not limits.

Next Steps

Now that you understand the power of budgeting, the next step is learning **how to make smart choices** with your money. That starts by understanding the difference between **wants** and **needs** — a skill that can make or break your financial future.

The Difference Between Wants and Needs

If you've ever wondered why your money disappears faster than you expected, there's a good chance it's because of this one thing: **you're spending too much on wants, thinking they're needs.**

Learning the difference between **wants** and **needs** is one of the most important financial skills you'll ever build. It's simple, but powerful — and it's a habit that will protect your wallet for life.

What Are Needs?

Needs are the things you must have to live, work, and stay healthy. Without them, your basic life can fall apart.

Common examples of **needs**:

- Rent or a place to live
- Groceries or basic food
- School supplies (if you're a student)
- A working phone (for communication, work, or class)
- Public transportation or gas to get to school or work
- Prescriptions or basic healthcare

These are **non-negotiable**. If you don't cover your needs, everything else becomes harder — you can't focus, work, study, or stay well.

Needs should always come **first** in your budget.

What Are Wants?

Wants are the things you enjoy, but can live without. They're optional — even if they feel important in the moment.

Common examples of **wants**:

- Coffee shop drinks or fast food
- Streaming subscriptions (Netflix, Spotify, etc.)
- New clothes when your current ones are fine
- Gaming upgrades or in-app purchases
- Concerts, movie tickets, or takeout
- The newest phone, laptop, or headphones

There's nothing wrong with spending money on wants — **as long as your needs are covered first.**

Think of wants as **rewards** — not requirements.

How to Tell the Difference

Here's a quick test:

If you lost your job tomorrow, would you still pay for it?

- **Yes?** Probably a **need**
- **No?** It's likely a **want**

Another test:

Will your health, safety, or education suffer without it?

- **Yes?** It's a need
- **No?** It's a want

Still unsure? Try this 3-part filter:

Ask Yourself	If the answer is "Yes"…
Do I need this to survive or function daily?	It's a **need**
Can I find a cheaper or free version?	Might be a **want**
Am I buying this because I'm bored or emotional?	Definitely a **want**

Real-World Example: Meet David

What happened:
David is a full-time student who works weekends at a grocery store. One month, he realized he had just $15 left in his account — and rent was due in four days.

What went wrong:
David thought he was budgeting. But he had mixed up wants and needs. He counted things like Uber rides, food delivery, and new shoes as "needs." Meanwhile, he had skipped saving for rent.

What we learn from it:
Without clearly separating wants from needs, David spent money on things he *liked*, instead of what he *had* to cover. After this wake-up call, he started listing his needs first and only spending on wants after the essentials were covered. He's now on top of his rent, and still has room for fun — just not all the time.

Why This Matters (Especially for Students)

If your income is small — and for most students it is — you don't have room for sloppy spending. Getting this one habit right will:

- Keep your bills paid on time
- Help you save up for bigger goals
- Give you real peace of mind
- Keep you from falling into debt early

Wants can wait. Needs can't.

Tactical Best Practices

- **List your needs before every payday:** Write down rent, food, transportation, phone — then see what's left.
- **Never use a credit card for wants:** If you can't pay cash for it, you shouldn't buy it yet.
- **Delay wants for 48 hours:** If you still want it after two days, it might be worth it — or not.
- **Use the "friend test":** Would you call a friend and say, "I *have* to spend $20 on this today"? If not, it's a want.

Common Pitfalls

- Calling something a need just because it's popular or trendy
- Convincing yourself you "deserve it" without checking your budget
- Failing to plan ahead for real needs, like school supplies or food
- Spending on wants first, then struggling to cover essentials

Checklist: Spotting Wants vs. Needs

☑ Look at your last 10 purchases
☑ Highlight which ones were absolute essentials
☑ Put a star next to anything that could have waited
☑ Calculate how much of your spending was on wants
☑ Set a new rule: Needs first, always

Conclusion
The difference between wants and needs might seem obvious, but most people get it wrong every day. If you build this habit now, you'll avoid unnecessary stress, save money faster, and make smarter choices without feeling guilty or deprived. It's not about saying no to everything — it's about saying yes to what *really matters first*.

Next Steps
Now that you can clearly separate wants from needs, it's time to learn how **technology — including AI — can help you budget smarter and faster.** In the next section, we'll show you how to use apps, tools, and smart features to take some of the pressure off managing money manually.

How AI Can Make Budgeting Easier

Let's face it — budgeting takes effort. You need to track your money, plan ahead, make decisions, and adjust when life changes. But the good news? **You don't have to do it all alone.**

Thanks to **AI (Artificial Intelligence),** budgeting is now faster, smarter, and more beginner-friendly than ever — even for students.

If you're using a phone, a bank app, or a money tool with smart features, chances are AI is already helping you in ways you didn't notice.

Let's break it down.

What Is AI (In Simple Terms)?

AI stands for **Artificial Intelligence** — it's technology that can think, learn, and make decisions like a human (but much faster).

In budgeting tools, AI watches your money patterns and helps you:

- Organize your income and spending
- Predict your future costs
- Warn you before you overspend
- Suggest better ways to use your money

You don't need to understand code or data science to benefit. You just need to **know how to use the right tools.**

How AI Makes Budgeting Easier (Without the Stress)

1. Automatic Spending Tracking

AI-powered apps connect to your bank and credit card accounts. They watch your transactions and automatically sort them into categories like:

- Food
- Transportation
- Entertainment
- Bills
- Shopping

You don't have to write it all down — the app does it for you.

✅ **Example:** You buy lunch at Chipotle. The app logs it under "Food" without you lifting a finger.

2. Smart Budget Suggestions

Based on your habits, income, and past spending, some AI tools will suggest a realistic monthly budget for you.

You don't have to guess. AI says:

- "You usually spend $100/month on takeout — let's cap it at $80 this month."
- "Your average phone bill is $65 — let's add that to your fixed expenses."

It learns from you and gives you **realistic, personalized goals**.

3. Spending Alerts and Notifications

AI can send you instant updates if something unusual happens:

- "You're spending more on food than usual this week."
- "You have a bill due tomorrow — make sure you have enough in your account."

These alerts help you **stay on track in real time**, so you don't go over budget without realizing it.

4. Visual Reports and Trends

AI can turn your money data into **easy-to-read charts and summaries.** No spreadsheets needed.

You'll see:

- Where your money is going (by category)
- How your spending is changing over time
- What your top spending habits are

Seeing it visually helps you make **faster, smarter decisions**.

5. Goal-Setting and Auto-Saving

Some apps use AI to help you set savings goals — and even move money automatically.

☑ **Example:** You set a goal to save $100 for textbooks. The app calculates how much you need to set aside each week — and helps you save it without thinking about it.

Some even round up your purchases (like from $4.75 to $5.00) and save the spare change toward your goal.

Real-World Example: Meet Malik

What happened:
Malik is a student with two part-time gigs and not much time. He struggled to keep up with his money manually — always forgetting to track spending and falling short by the end of the month.

What changed:
He downloaded a budgeting app with AI features. The app tracked his spending automatically, warned him when he was overspending on delivery food, and helped him build a $200 emergency fund in two months — just by setting small weekly goals.

What we learn from it:
AI isn't just for tech geeks. When used right, it can help busy students like Malik take control of their money — even if they don't have time to budget every day.

Tactical Best Practices

- **Use an AI-based budgeting app** like Cleo, YNAB, Monarch, or Rocket Money
- **Link your bank accounts safely** — this is what allows AI to work in real-time
- **Set savings goals** and let the app track your progress
- **Turn on alerts** for spending limits, bills, and goals
- **Review your weekly money report** to see what changed

Common Mistakes to Avoid

- Thinking AI will do *everything* for you — you still need to check in
- Ignoring alerts and notifications — they're meant to help you course-correct
- Not reviewing your spending trends — insights only help if you use them
- Over-trusting predictions — AI is smart, but your judgment still matters

Checklist: Let AI Help You Budget Smarter

- ☑ Choose a budgeting app with AI features
- ☑ Link your main spending accounts
- ☑ Set one simple savings goal (e.g., $10/week)
- ☑ Turn on alerts for bills and categories
- ☑ Check your app once a week — treat it like a money coach

Conclusion

AI makes budgeting easier, faster, and way less stressful. You don't need to be a financial expert or track every penny by hand. With the right tools, you can get insights, stay organized, and grow your savings — even if you're starting small.

Technology can't replace your judgment, but it can **support your decisions** and keep you consistent. And when it comes to money, consistency beats perfection every time.

CHAPTER 2

Knowing Your Money

What Is Income? (Jobs, Allowances, Gifts)

Before you can build a budget, make smart choices, or start saving money — you need to know exactly what's coming **in**. That's your **income**.

Think of income as your **money supply**. It's the cash that flows **into your life**, and it's what you use to pay for everything else.

No matter how big or small, **every dollar you receive counts as income.**

Definition: What Exactly Is Income?

Income is any money you receive — regularly or occasionally — from any source.

If it adds to your bank account, wallet, or cash stash, it's income. Simple as that.

Common Sources of Income for Students

You don't need a full-time job to have income. Here are the most common ways students and young adults receive money:

1. Jobs (Part-Time or Full-Time)

- Working at a coffee shop, retail store, restaurant, or freelancing
- Paid internships or campus jobs
- Babysitting, tutoring, mowing lawns

If you're working for someone and getting paid — that's income.

2. Allowances

- Weekly or monthly money from parents or guardians
- Often tied to chores or school performance (but not always)
- May come in cash or through apps like Venmo or bank transfers

Even if it feels like a "gift," if it's regular, it's part of your income.

3. Gifts or One-Time Money

- Birthday or holiday cash
- Graduation money
- Random transfers from relatives ("Just because" money)

These are not guaranteed or predictable, but they still count as income when they happen.

4. Scholarships or Student Aid (with spending allowance)

- If a scholarship gives you extra funds for books, meals, or personal use — that counts
- Refunds from student loans or grants after tuition is paid

If you can **spend** the money, it's income — even if it came from school.

Real-World Example: Meet Aria

What happened:
Aria is a full-time college student who works 10 hours a week at the campus library, earning $400/month. Her parents also send her $100/month for food and transit, and she got $150 in birthday money from her grandparents last month.

What went right:
Aria didn't assume her job was her only income. She wrote down **every source** — even the birthday money — so she could budget it properly. That one-time gift helped her cover textbook costs she hadn't expected.

What we learn from it:
Tracking **all** sources of income — even small or random ones — helps you make better decisions and avoid surprises. Aria was able to stay on track by knowing exactly what money was available.

Why Income Awareness Matters

If you don't know **how much money you actually have**, you'll overspend — or hold back when you could afford something smart. Knowing your income helps you:

- Set a realistic budget
- Know what you can afford
- Avoid relying on credit or borrowing
- Start saving without guessing
- Make confident financial decisions

Tactical Best Practices

- **Track your income in one place:** Use a notes app, spreadsheet, or journal
- **Separate regular income from one-time money:** Plan based on the money you can count on
- **Don't forget digital income:** CashApp, Venmo, PayPal — it all counts
- **Check your bank deposits:** If your job uses direct deposit, check for accuracy every payday

Common Mistakes to Avoid

- Only counting job income and forgetting about allowances or gifts
- Spending gift money immediately without budgeting it
- Assuming income will always stay the same (hours can change!)
- Not tracking income at all — "I think I have around $300" isn't good enough

Checklist: Know Your Income

- ☑ List all your income sources
- ☑ Note how often you receive each one (weekly, monthly, one-time)
- ☑ Add them up for a total monthly income
- ☑ Mark any income that's not guaranteed next month
- ☑ Use this number as your budget starting point

Conclusion

Income is the starting point of every smart financial decision. Whether you're making $100 or $1,000 a month, knowing exactly where your money comes from puts you in control. You can't plan what you don't measure.

What Are Expenses? (Food, Rent, Phone Bill)

If income is the money coming in, **expenses** are the money going out.

Understanding your **expenses** is just as important — maybe even more important — than understanding your income. Because no matter how much you make, if you spend it all (or more), you'll always feel like you're broke.

Let's break it down, simply and clearly.

What Exactly Are Expenses?

Expenses are anything you spend money on.
If money leaves your wallet, bank account, or digital app — that's an expense.

There are two main types of expenses:

- **Fixed expenses** — the same amount every month
- **Variable expenses** — amounts that change from week to week or month to month

Knowing the difference helps you plan better, avoid surprises, and stay in control.

Common Student Expenses (With Examples)

Let's look at some everyday examples, so you know what to watch for:

Fixed Expenses

These are the "must-pay" items — same amount, usually every month.

- Rent or dorm fees
- Phone bill
- Internet subscription
- Monthly transit pass
- Gym membership
- Student loan payment (if you've started repayment)

You can usually plan ahead for these because they don't change much. These should be listed **first** in your budget.

Variable Expenses

These are flexible and change based on your habits, choices, or events.

- Groceries or takeout food
- Gas or rideshare costs
- School supplies
- Entertainment (movies, concerts, games)
- Clothes or shoes
- Gifts for friends or family

These can sneak up on you. You need to **track them weekly**, or they'll drain your budget without you noticing.

Real-World Example: Meet Zoe

What happened:
Zoe is a university student who earns $800/month from a part-time job. She thought that would be enough. But by the third week of every month, she was short on cash — even though she wasn't "buying anything crazy."

What went wrong:
Zoe only looked at her fixed expenses: $400 rent, $70 phone bill, $50 bus pass. She didn't realize her variable expenses — like $100 on takeout, $80 on clothes, and $90 on spontaneous weekend activities — were pushing her way over budget.

What we learn from it:
If you don't include **all** your expenses, especially the small ones, your budget won't work. Zoe started tracking every expense and cut back on food delivery — instantly saving $60/month.

Why Expenses Matter More Than You Think

If you don't track your expenses, you won't know:

- Where your money is really going
- What you're overspending on
- Where you can cut back
- How much you have left to save

Most people don't need to earn more — they just need to **spend better.**

Tactical Best Practices

- **Track every expense, no matter how small:** $3 on coffee matters if you do it 10 times.
- **Write down your fixed expenses at the start of the month:** These are your "non-negotiables."
- **Review your variable expenses weekly:** Find patterns (weekend spending spikes, anyone?).
- **Use categories in a budgeting app:** Let it organize food, rent, bills, and fun for you.
- **Adjust, don't guess:** If your spending is off track, make changes early — not when you're broke.

Common Mistakes to Avoid

- Only budgeting for big expenses like rent or tuition
- Forgetting about monthly subscriptions that autopay (they add up!)
- Ignoring small daily spending like snacks, rideshares, or "quick" online orders
- Treating fun spending like it's "free" money — it's not

Checklist: Manage Your Expenses Like a Pro

- ☑ List your monthly fixed expenses
- ☑ Estimate your weekly variable expenses
- ☑ Track every expense for at least 30 days
- ☑ Find the category where you overspend most
- ☑ Make a spending limit for that category next month
- ☑ Repeat and refine — budgeting is a habit, not a one-time task

Conclusion

Expenses are where most budgets fall apart — not because people are irresponsible, but because they don't track what's really going out. Once you understand your expenses clearly, you'll see exactly what's stealing your money — and how to stop it.

Managing expenses doesn't mean cutting out all the fun. It means **choosing what matters most and staying in control.**

Good vs. Bad Spending Habits

Every dollar you spend is a decision. And over time, those decisions turn into **habits** — either smart, helpful habits that build your future, or risky, draining habits that leave you stressed and broke.

Here's the good news: you don't need to be perfect with money to be successful. But you do need to build more **good spending habits** than bad ones — and start doing it now, while your financial life is still simple.

What Are Spending Habits?

Spending habits are the regular ways you choose to use your money — often without thinking.

For example:

- Do you always buy coffee before class, even if you have coffee at home?
- Do you check your balance before buying something, or only after?
- Do you wait for sales, or buy things immediately?

These patterns shape your financial future — whether you notice them or not.

Good Spending Habits (That Help You)

These habits keep your money organized, intentional, and under your control — even if you're not earning much yet.

1. Tracking Before Spending

Good spenders **check their balance or budget first** before making a purchase. They know what they can afford and don't guess.

2. Comparing Prices or Waiting for Sales

Instead of impulse buying, they **pause** and ask, "Can I get this cheaper somewhere else?" or "Can it wait?"

3. Spending With a Purpose

They don't spend because they're bored or stressed. They spend because it's something they actually need or truly value.

4. Setting Limits for Fun Spending

They give themselves **freedom with structure** — for example: "I'll spend $40 a month on entertainment and stick to it."

5. Paying Bills or Saving First

They handle their **musts** first — like rent, phone bill, or savings goals — before they treat themselves.

Bad Spending Habits (That Hurt You)

These are habits that feel harmless at first but slowly drain your money and increase stress over time.

1. Spending Without Checking

Buying things without knowing how much money you have can lead to overdraft fees or going into debt.

2. Emotional or Boredom Shopping

If you spend money just to feel better or to kill time, you're not in control — your emotions are.

3. Overusing Credit for Non-Essentials

Swiping a credit card for fast food, gaming, or clothes might feel easy — until the bill comes with interest.

4. Ignoring Small Purchases

"I only spent $5" can add up fast. Ten $5 purchases in a week is $50. Multiply that by a month, and you're losing serious cash.

5. Not Reviewing Past Spending

If you never look at where your money went last week or last month, you'll keep repeating the same mistakes.

Real-World Example: Meet Lucas and Sam

What happened:
Lucas and Sam are roommates. Both work part-time and earn about the same each month. But by the third week, Lucas always runs out of money — while Sam still has enough to save.

What went wrong (for Lucas):
Lucas spends without checking his balance. He grabs food delivery multiple times a week and buys things on impulse. He doesn't track where his money goes — and ends up short.

What went right (for Sam):
Sam tracks her spending with an app. She gives herself a fun spending limit, waits for sales, and always pays her bills first. She still treats herself — but she plans for it.

What we learn:
The difference wasn't how much they made — it was how they **used** it. Habits are everything.

Tactical Best Practices

- **Use spending alerts or limits:** Many budgeting apps let you set category limits and notify you if you go over.
- **Pause before buying:** Ask yourself, "Do I really need this right now? Can it wait?"
- **Review your last 30 days of spending:** Find the top 3 things you spend on — and decide if they're worth it.
- **Talk to a friend about money goals:** Accountability helps build better habits.

Common Pitfalls to Avoid

- Saying "it's just $10" too often
- Assuming good intentions are enough — habits need systems
- Treating fun spending as "outside" your budget
- Copying other people's habits without knowing if they're struggling too
- Thinking you'll "start budgeting next month" — start now, even if it's messy

Checklist: Build Better Spending Habits

☑ Track everything you spend for one week
☑ Pick one habit to improve (like checking your balance first)
☑ Set a fun spending limit and stick to it
☑ Find one thing you can delay buying this week
☑ Reward yourself with something **planned** — not impulsive

Conclusion
Your spending habits shape your entire financial life — not just today, but for years to come. Building even one or two **good habits** now can make saving easier, paying bills stress-free, and reaching your goals feel realistic.

Money doesn't just disappear — **habits direct it.** Make sure your habits are working for you, not against you.

AI Apps That Track Your Spending Automatically

Budgeting doesn't have to mean writing down every dollar in a notebook or doing math after every purchase. In fact, **you can let smart apps do the heavy lifting for you.** Thanks to Artificial Intelligence (AI), there are now tools that **track your spending in real time, categorize it automatically, and alert you before things go off track.**

Whether you're a student managing your first part-time paycheck or just trying to stop wondering where your money went, these apps act like a **personal money assistant — in your pocket.**

Let's look at how these AI-powered tools work, and which ones are actually worth using.

How Do AI Budgeting Apps Work?

Most of these apps connect securely to your bank account, debit card, or credit card. Once connected, the app uses **AI to analyze your transactions**, sort them into categories, and help you make sense of your money.

They don't just record what you spent — they **learn** your habits, and help you make better choices.

AI apps can:

- Show where your money is going
- Group spending into categories (like food, rent, or shopping)
- Spot patterns (like weekly overspending)
- Send alerts when you're close to your budget
- Recommend changes to help you save more

It's budgeting made smart, not hard.

Top AI-Powered Spending Tracker Apps for Beginners

These apps are beginner-friendly, student-ready, and loaded with AI features. Most have free versions, and all are designed to make budgeting as painless as possible.

☑ Cleo

Best for: Fun, conversational budgeting (perfect for students)
AI feature: You can *chat* with Cleo like a money coach. Ask it how much you spent on food last week, and it will tell you instantly.

- Tracks spending and categories
- Roasts you when you overspend (funny, but useful)
- Lets you set savings goals with automation
- Shows a full breakdown of your habits

💡 *Why it's great:* Cleo makes money management feel like texting a smart, sarcastic friend who's got your back.

☑ Rocket Money

Best for: Managing subscriptions and recurring bills
AI feature: Automatically finds hidden subscriptions, tracks recurring charges, and alerts you before they hit.

- Categorizes spending and shows your cash flow
- Cancels unwanted subscriptions with a tap
- Gives alerts for upcoming bills
- Offers smart budgeting insights

💡 *Why it's great:* It's like having a radar that spots money leaks you didn't even notice.

✅ Monarch Money

Best for: Full budgeting overview with shared access
AI feature: Organizes your accounts and spending history into clear visuals. Learns your habits and makes personalized suggestions.

- Great for building a monthly budget
- Beautiful dashboards and charts
- Helps you track savings and goals
- Can invite a partner or roommate to manage shared expenses

💡 *Why it's great:* It's simple, powerful, and helpful for visual learners who want to see their whole money picture.

✅ You Need a Budget (YNAB)

Best for: Students who want to master budgeting, not just track it
AI feature: Learns your income and spending cycles, and helps you assign every dollar a job. It's not just about watching your money — it helps you plan with purpose.

- Helps you avoid paycheck-to-paycheck stress
- Builds habits like delayed spending and emergency saving
- Has a strong educational side with videos and courses

💡 *Why it's great:* YNAB turns you into someone who *controls* their money, not just watches it disappear.

✅ Simplifi by Quicken

Best for: Real-time cash flow tracking
AI feature: Predicts your future balance based on past spending and upcoming bills

- Live updates of your money
- Daily breakdowns by category
- Monthly reports and projections

- Personalized insights on how to save

💡 *Why it's great:* It helps you see problems *before* they happen — not after you're already short.

Real-World Example: Meet Leila

What happened:
Leila is a college student juggling a campus job and part-time babysitting. She felt overwhelmed trying to keep up with her spending. She'd often say, "I thought I had more money than this."

What changed:
She installed Cleo. The app started tracking every expense, showed her she was spending over $100/month on snacks and rideshares, and helped her set a "fun budget" cap. After two months, she had saved $160 without cutting out the things she loved — just by being more aware.

What we learn:
With the right AI app, budgeting doesn't feel like work. It feels like **clarity.**

Tactical Best Practices

- **Link your bank accounts securely** — that's how the app learns your real habits
- **Turn on notifications** for spending alerts and category limits
- **Set one small savings goal** (like $10/week) and let the app help you track it
- **Review your spending weekly** using the app's smart reports
- **Let it spot subscriptions or "quiet" spending** you forgot about

Common Pitfalls to Avoid

- Ignoring app alerts or advice — the AI only helps if you listen
- Using too many apps at once — pick one and stick with it
- Not checking the app until it's too late
- Relying on the app but still overspending "just a little" — small leaks sink ships

Checklist: Start With AI Budgeting Today

☑ Pick ONE app that fits your personality and needs
☑ Link your main spending account(s)
☑ Set category alerts (like Food, Fun, or Transport)
☑ Check your spending breakdown at the end of each week
☑ Adjust next month's spending plan based on insights

Conclusion

AI apps make it easier than ever to take control of your money. They work quietly in the background — tracking, sorting, alerting, and suggesting — so you can stay in charge without doing all the work yourself.

Budgeting used to be a chore. Now, it's a smart system — powered by tools that actually help you spend better, save faster, and feel in control.

CHAPTER 3

Simple Budget Rules

The 50/30/20 Rule Explained Simply

If you're just starting out with budgeting and want an easy way to organize your money, the **50/30/20 rule** is one of the best places to begin.

It's simple. It works. And it helps you **balance spending, saving, and living your life** — without needing a finance degree.

What Is the 50/30/20 Rule?

It's a way to divide your income into three clear categories:

- **50% for Needs**
- **30% for Wants**
- **20% for Savings and Debt Payments**

Think of your money like a pizza. This rule slices it into three smart pieces, so you don't overspend on one area and starve another.

Why Use This Rule?

- It's **easy to follow** (no complicated math)
- It works no matter your income
- It helps you spend with purpose, not just by habit
- It builds healthy money habits early

Whether you're a student making $400 a month or $2,000, the rule adjusts automatically. It's a flexible guide — not a strict limit.

Let's Break Down Each Piece:

50% – Needs

This is your **must-pay** stuff. These are the basics you can't live without.

Common **needs**:

- Rent or housing
- Groceries
- Public transport, gas, or ride-share
- Phone bill
- Basic school supplies
- Insurance or medical costs

💡 *Important:* Needs are *survival*, not *comfort*. Fast food isn't a need. Wi-Fi for school might be.

30% – Wants

This is your **fun and flexible** money. These things make life enjoyable — but you could live without them if needed.

Common **wants**:

- Dining out or takeout
- New clothes (if not essential)
- Streaming services (Netflix, Spotify)
- Video games, concerts, hobbies
- Upgraded tech or accessories

This part of your budget keeps you from feeling restricted — you get to enjoy life *without* wrecking your finances.

20% – Savings and Debt Payments

This is your **future-proofing** money. It's what keeps you safe, prepared, and moving forward.

Use this part to:

- Build an emergency fund
- Save for school supplies, travel, or big purchases
- Pay down credit card debt (if any)
- Start investing later on

Even saving **$10 a week** counts. The key is building the habit early.

Real-World Example: Meet Ben

What happened:
Ben is a student who earns $900/month working part-time. He never budgeted before and always felt like money disappeared too fast.

What changed:
Ben used the 50/30/20 rule to divide his income:

- **$450 for needs**: rent, groceries, bus pass
- **$270 for wants**: going out, games, subscriptions
- **$180 for savings**: building an emergency fund

By sticking close to those numbers, Ben finally felt in control — and even had money left at the end of the month.

What we learn:
The rule gave Ben structure *and* freedom. He didn't have to track every dollar, just keep the balance right.

How to Use the Rule in 3 Easy Steps

1. **Know your total income**
   → Add up what you earn or receive monthly
2. **Multiply by the percentages**
   → 50% for needs, 30% for wants, 20% for savings/debt
3. **Plug in real numbers**
   → Assign actual expenses to each category

Here's an example if you make **$1,000/month**:

Category	Amount	Examples
50% Needs	$500	Rent, food, transport, phone
30% Wants	$300	Takeout, movies, Spotify
20% Savings/Debt	$200	Emergency fund, paying off debt

It's that simple.

Tactical Best Practices

- **Use the rule as a guide, not a cage:** Life happens. Adjust when needed.
- **Review your real expenses:** Some people think they're spending 30% on wants — but it's really 50%.
- **Use budgeting apps to divide categories:** Many apps support this format by default.
- **Start with savings, not leftovers:** Pay yourself first. Even a small amount builds momentum.

Common Mistakes to Avoid

- Counting wants as needs (yes, that daily latte counts)
- Forgetting to include small subscriptions in the "wants" category
- Skipping the savings part — even $10/month matters
- Thinking the rule has to be exact — it's a **guide**, not a test

Checklist: Try the 50/30/20 Rule This Month

☑ Add up your total monthly income
☑ Multiply it by 0.5, 0.3, and 0.2 to get category targets
☑ List your needs, wants, and savings goals under each
☑ Track your real spending for 30 days
☑ Adjust next month to improve balance

Conclusion

The 50/30/20 rule is one of the simplest, most beginner-friendly ways to start budgeting. It gives you structure, flexibility, and a clear path to saving — without making you feel restricted. You're still in control, but now with **intentional balance.**

Use it once, and you'll wonder how you ever lived without it.

Essentials First: Food, Shelter, Transport

When it comes to managing your money — especially on a tight budget — you need to **prioritize what matters most.**

No matter how much (or how little) you earn, the smartest financial move you can make is simple:

Cover your essentials first. Always.

Essentials are your **foundation** — the things you truly need to stay safe, healthy, and able to function in school or work. Without these, everything else in your life starts to fall apart.

What Are Essentials?

Essentials are things you *must* have to live and keep going day to day. They're not optional, and they come **before** fun spending, shopping, or extras.

For students and young adults, the three core essentials are:

1. Food (Groceries and Basic Meals)

You need energy to study, work, and live. That means **real food**, not just snacks or soda.

Examples of essential food expenses:

- Groceries for the week
- Campus meal plans (if required)
- Basic kitchen supplies (bread, rice, eggs, etc.)
- Occasional low-cost takeout (if it replaces a full meal)

💡 *Pro Tip:* Eating out for fun is a **want**. But eating to stay nourished is a **need**.

2. Shelter (Rent, Utilities, Dorm Fees)

You need a place to live — and it must be stable, safe, and predictable.

Essential shelter expenses include:

- Rent or dorm payments
- Electricity, water, and basic utilities
- Heating or cooling (especially in extreme climates)
- Shared household costs (if you split with roommates)

💡 *Pro Tip:* Always budget rent **first**. It's usually your biggest monthly expense, and missing a payment can lead to serious problems.

3. Transport (To School, Work, or Essentials)

If you can't get to class or your job, the rest of your budget won't matter.

Essential transportation includes:

- Public transit passes (bus, train, metro)
- Gas money (if you drive)
- Occasional rideshare for emergencies
- Basic bike maintenance (if you cycle)

♀ *Pro Tip:* Transport is essential only when it helps you **function** — not just for fun or convenience.

Real-World Example: Meet Ryan

What happened:
Ryan is a college sophomore with a part-time tutoring job. He got his paycheck and spent half of it on new clothes and concert tickets. Later in the month, he struggled to afford groceries and had to borrow money for rent.

What went wrong:
Ryan didn't put essentials first. He treated wants like priorities — and his **needs suffered for it**.

What we learn:
By prioritizing food, shelter, and transport at the **start of the month**, Ryan could have covered his essentials without stress — and still had room for a few extras.

Why Prioritizing Essentials Is Critical

- Helps you avoid emergencies and last-minute borrowing
- Keeps you healthy, safe, and able to work or study
- Reduces stress and anxiety about money
- Builds discipline and smarter long-term habits

It's not about saying no to everything else. It's about **saying yes to the things that matter most — first.**

Tactical Best Practices

- **List your essentials before the month begins:** Write down exact amounts for food, rent, and transport.
- **Set that money aside first:** Before you spend anything else.
- **Estimate your weekly food costs** and keep track — groceries are more controllable than eating out.
- **Don't dip into essential money** for impulse buys or social plans.

Common Mistakes to Avoid

- Spending on wants before needs — then scrambling later
- Underestimating how much you spend on food or gas
- Forgetting to plan for monthly bills like rent or electricity
- Assuming you'll "figure it out" later — it rarely works

Checklist: Cover Essentials First

- ☑ List your exact rent or housing cost
- ☑ Estimate weekly food budget (grocery + meals)
- ☑ Add transport costs (bus pass, gas, etc.)
- ☑ Total these amounts before spending on anything else
- ☑ Set aside or track those funds first in your budget app or notebook

Conclusion

Budgeting isn't just about cutting back — it's about **putting the right things first**. And nothing comes before the basics: food, shelter, and transport. Once those are covered, you can start looking at wants, savings, and goals. But **without these three, everything else falls apart.**

Taking care of essentials gives you stability, peace of mind, and a solid foundation — no matter how much money you're working with.

Savings and Fun Money Balance

Saving money is smart. Having fun is also important.
The real challenge? **Balancing both** — without letting one destroy the other.

Too much saving with zero enjoyment can lead to burnout. Too much fun with no saving? That leads to stress and debt.
The goal is a healthy middle ground where you're **building your future** *and* still **enjoying your present.**

This is where the concept of **"Savings and Fun Money Balance"** comes in — a simple way to give both parts of your life the space they deserve.

What Is "Fun Money"?

Fun money is the part of your budget you set aside for things you enjoy — the *wants*, not the *needs*.

It's the money you use for:

- Going out with friends
- Ordering takeout or coffee
- Buying clothes you like (not just need)
- Hobbies, games, or streaming subscriptions
- Treats, gadgets, concerts, or weekend trips

Fun money isn't wasteful — **it's planned freedom.** The key is setting a limit **before** you start spending.

What Is Savings?

Savings is money you set aside on purpose — not to spend now, but to prepare for later.

There are different kinds of savings:

- **Emergency savings** – for unexpected costs (like medical bills, car trouble, etc.)
- **Short-term savings** – for things like textbooks, travel, gifts, or tuition fees
- **Long-term savings** – for bigger goals like moving out, buying a car, or starting your adult life

Even $5–$10 per week can grow into something real over time. What matters is **consistency, not size.**

Why You Need Both

Some people say: *"Just save everything."* Others say: *"You're young — enjoy it while you can."*

Both are wrong.

You need to save **enough** to feel secure — but also spend **enough** to enjoy your life now.

The healthiest budget includes both:
Discipline + Joy
Responsibility + Freedom

Real-World Example: Meet Jordan

What happened:
Jordan is a student who started budgeting aggressively. He put 100% of his extra money into savings. No takeout, no movie nights, no fun. After three months, he gave up, overspent, and wiped out half his savings in one weekend.

What went wrong:
Jordan didn't give himself **any room to breathe.** Saving everything sounded noble, but it wasn't sustainable. It led to frustration and a spending rebound.

What we learn:
You need a **realistic plan** that includes both saving and spending on yourself. Without fun money, budgeting feels like punishment — and punishment never lasts.

How to Balance Savings and Fun Money

Here's a simple starting point, especially if you're following the **50/30/20 rule**:

- 20% of your income = **Savings or debt payoff**
- 30% of your income = **Wants (aka fun money)**

If you earn $1,000/month:

- Save **$200**
- Spend up to **$300** on fun — guilt-free, because you planned it

💡 *Tip:* If your income is low, shift the balance slightly — just **don't skip savings entirely.** Even saving **$5/week** builds the habit.

Tactical Best Practices

- **Set a weekly fun money limit** (e.g., $40/week) — and stick to it
- **Automate your savings** so it's gone before you can spend it
- **Label your savings goals**: "Emergency Fund," "New Laptop," "Spring Break" — this keeps it exciting
- **Use cash or prepaid cards for fun money** to avoid overspending

Common Mistakes to Avoid

- Saving so much that you feel restricted (and give up)
- Spending "extra" money without a plan — it's fun until it's gone
- Using credit cards for fun money — turns short-term joy into long-term debt
- Not tracking fun money spending — it disappears fast if you're not watching

Checklist: Balance Your Budget for Life and Fun

- ☑ Set a realistic monthly savings target
- ☑ Decide how much you can spend guilt-free on fun
- ☑ Track both using an app or notes
- ☑ Adjust monthly based on how it feels — too tight? Too loose?
- ☑ Celebrate wins (like saving $100 or sticking to your fun budget)

Conclusion

Balancing savings and fun money isn't about being perfect — it's about being **intentional.**

You deserve to enjoy your life now **and** build a future you'll be proud of. With the right plan, you don't have to choose one or the other.

Start small, stay consistent, and give yourself room to grow — and room to live.

How AI Tools Suggest Better Rules for You

Budgeting is personal. What works for someone else might not work for you — especially if your income changes, your spending is inconsistent, or you're just starting out.

That's where **AI tools** shine. Instead of forcing you into a one-size-fits-all budget, AI can **study your money habits** and **suggest rules** that actually fit your lifestyle.

Think of AI as your **personal finance coach** — not just telling you what to do, but learning how *you* live and adjusting the rules to match.

What Are "Budget Rules"?

Budget rules are simple guidelines that help you decide:

- How much to spend on different things (food, fun, savings)
- When to stop spending in a certain category
- How much to save from each paycheck
- How to stay on track without feeling restricted

A popular example is the **50/30/20 rule** — but AI can create or tweak rules based on *your* real life.

How AI Tools Build Better Rules (Step-by-Step)

Here's how smart budgeting apps with AI learn and suggest rules for you:

1. They Watch Your Habits

Once you link your bank account, AI watches:

- What you spend (and where)
- How often money comes in
- Which categories you overspend in
- What days or weeks you tend to spend more

2. They Find Patterns

AI can spot things you don't:

- You spend more on weekends
- You always go over budget on food
- You get paid biweekly but spend like it's weekly

This lets the app **adjust advice** to fit your rhythms — not random averages.

3. They Suggest Smart Rules

After learning your habits, AI tools can recommend custom rules like:

- "Spend no more than $60/week on takeout"
- "Save $15 every Friday automatically"
- "Cut ride-share trips after $40/month"
- "Only spend fun money after bills are paid"

These rules are based on **you**, not a generic budget plan.

4. They Adjust as You Change

Life changes — income goes up or down, you move, your needs shift.
AI updates your rules as it notices changes:

- You get a new job? The savings rule increases.
- Spending on books this month? It adjusts other categories.
- Missed a savings goal? It resets a lower target to keep you motivated.

It's not just smart — it's flexible.

Real-World Example: Meet Priya

What happened:
Priya is a student who downloaded a budgeting app to get control over her money. She tried to use the 50/30/20 rule but always overspent on takeout and under-saved.

What changed:
Her app noticed that she spent around $80/month more than planned on food. It suggested a custom rule: "Cap takeout at $15/week and save $10 every Sunday." She followed it — and not only hit her savings goal for the first time, but still enjoyed her favorite meals.

What we learn:
AI isn't about being strict — it's about being smart. Priya didn't need to spend less — she needed better structure. AI gave her rules she could actually follow.

Examples of AI-Generated Budget Rules

AI Tool Suggestion	What It Means
"Round up every purchase and save the difference"	Turns spare change into automatic savings
"Delay non-essential purchases for 24 hours"	Helps reduce impulse spending
"Set a weekly limit on entertainment at $25"	Keeps fun spending in check
"Freeze spending in shopping category for 7 days"	A soft restriction after overspending
"Auto-transfer $10 to savings after payday"	Builds savings into your routine

These kinds of rules **create structure without stress.** You're not guessing — you're guided.

Tactical Best Practices

- **Use AI apps with rule customization** (like Cleo, YNAB, or Simplifi)
- **Let the app run for a few weeks before applying changes** — give it time to learn you
- **Try one rule at a time** — don't overload yourself
- **Review rules monthly** to see what's working
- **Use AI to set *soft limits* — not punishments**

Common Mistakes to Avoid

- Ignoring the app's suggestions because they seem too simple
- Turning off alerts or weekly reports
- Expecting instant results — rules work best with **consistency**
- Sticking with a rule that doesn't fit your real life — it's okay to adjust

Checklist: Let AI Build Smarter Rules for You

☑ Use a budgeting app that tracks and analyzes spending
☑ Link your main bank and/or credit card accounts
☑ Let it track your habits for 2–4 weeks
☑ Accept and test 1–2 suggested rules
☑ Adjust if needed — or ask the app for new suggestions
☑ Review how those rules helped or didn't each month

Conclusion
You don't need to invent the perfect budget on your own. AI can take the guesswork out of money management by **creating personalized rules** that fit your real habits and goals — not someone else's.

It's like getting a financial coach that works quietly in the background, always watching, always improving your plan — just for you.

CHAPTER 4

Saving Made Easy

Why Saving Even $1 Matters

You might think saving money only counts when it's a big amount — like $100, $500, or more. But here's the truth most people miss:

Saving even $1 can change everything.

It's not about the number. It's about the **habit**.
Because if you can learn to save $1, you can eventually save $100.
And if you never start small, you'll never get to big.

The Power of Small Starts

You don't need to wait until you "have extra" to begin saving. In fact, people who wait for the "perfect time" to save often **never start at all**.

Saving $1:

- Builds the habit
- Builds confidence
- Builds momentum

It trains your brain to *think differently* about money. Suddenly, instead of spending every dollar, you start looking for ways to keep more.

Let's Do the Math

Saving $1 per day might not sound like much, but look at what it adds up to:

Daily Savings	Total in 1 Month	Total in 1 Year
$1/day	$30	$365
$2/day	$60	$730
$5/day	$150	$1,825

That's **over $1,800 a year** from just saving $5 a day — which is less than most takeout meals.

And it all starts with $1.

Real-World Example: Meet Nia

What happened:
Nia is a college student who thought she couldn't save. "My paychecks barely cover my bills," she told herself. Then one day, she tried something new — saving just $1 a day into a separate account.

What changed:
By the end of the first month, she had $30. The next month, she added $2/day. After six months, she had enough saved to buy a used laptop — *without using credit*.

What we learn:
The amount wasn't the key — the habit was. Saving just a little made Nia feel confident, capable, and in control. That feeling grew with every dollar.

Why It Matters for Students (Especially)

- You might not have big income right now — but you **do** have the power to start
- Learning to save early helps you **avoid debt later**
- It builds **financial discipline** that most adults never learn
- It proves to yourself that you're **in charge of your money**, not the other way around

Tactical Best Practices

- **Start with a number you won't miss** — even $0.50/day is enough to build momentum
- **Use an app or auto-transfer** to move money daily or weekly into savings
- **Give your savings a purpose** — label it "Emergency," "Tech Fund," or "Weekend Trip"
- **Track your progress visually** — use a chart, app, or sticky note on your desk

Common Pitfalls to Avoid

- Saying "it's not enough to matter" — *it always matters*
- Skipping saving because you had a tight week — save a smaller amount instead
- Waiting for a raise or extra income before starting
- Using savings as a backup checking account — treat it as **untouchable** unless needed

Checklist: Build the $1 Savings Habit

- [x] Choose a starting amount: $1/day or $5/week
- [x] Pick a savings goal to stay motivated
- [x] Set up automatic transfers or a daily reminder
- [x] Track your total each week — even if it's small
- [x] Increase the amount slowly over time

Conclusion

Saving money isn't about big leaps — it's about small steps taken **consistently**. That first $1 proves you're someone who thinks ahead, someone who takes action, and someone who builds security one day at a time.

Start now. Start small. And keep going — your future self will thank you.

Emergency Savings Explained

What would you do if your phone suddenly broke?
Or if your car wouldn't start the day before a final exam?
Or if you lost your job or your roommate moved out?

Emergencies happen — even when you're young, broke, or "just a student." And when they do, you need more than just good intentions. You need **emergency savings.**

Emergency savings is your financial safety net.
It keeps one small crisis from turning into a big disaster.

Let's break down what it is, how much you need, and how to build it — even if you're starting from zero.

What Is Emergency Savings?

Emergency savings is money you set aside to cover unexpected costs that you didn't plan for — but need to handle right away.

It's not for shopping, travel, or nights out. It's for when **life throws you a curveball**.

Common emergency expenses include:

- Medical or dental bills
- Car repairs or bike replacements
- Phone or laptop breakdowns
- Last-minute travel (family emergency, etc.)
- Rent gap if your roommate moves out
- Job loss or missed paycheck

Emergency savings is **not** for:

- Concert tickets
- Clothes
- Takeout or delivery
- Upgrades or "treat yourself" days

💡 *If you can plan for it, it's not an emergency.*

Why It Matters (Even for Students)

Many people think emergency funds are only for adults with kids, cars, or mortgages. But that's wrong. **Students need it just as much — maybe more.**

Here's why:

- You're more likely to live paycheck to paycheck
- You might not have family nearby to help
- You may not have access to credit or loans
- A small surprise cost could mean missing rent, meals, or class

Even saving **a little** emergency money can turn a crisis into a problem you can actually handle.

Real-World Example: Meet Mia

What happened:
Mia is a first-year college student who dropped her phone and broke the screen. Repair cost: $150. She didn't have the money, and her phone was her only internet access for school.

What went wrong:
Mia hadn't saved anything for emergencies. She had to borrow from three friends, skip a few meals, and wait two weeks to get it fixed — missing assignments along the way.

What we learn:
If Mia had even **$100 set aside**, she could've fixed the phone immediately and avoided the stress and missed work. After that month, she started putting away $10/week — and hasn't needed to borrow since.

How Much Should You Save?

If you're a student or just starting out, your emergency fund doesn't have to be huge. Here's a good starting range:

Starter Goal: $250–$500

Enough to cover:

- A basic car repair
- A broken phone screen
- A last-minute bus ticket or ride home
- A week of groceries

Bigger Goal: 1 Month of Expenses

If you're ready to level up, try saving **one full month of rent + food + transportation**.
This gives you breathing room for bigger emergencies like job loss or missed paychecks.

💡 *Start small. Build over time. Don't wait for a "perfect" moment.*

Where Should You Keep Emergency Savings?

- **Separate savings account:** Easy to access, harder to "accidentally" spend
- **Banking app with vault or bucket features:** Keeps emergency money away from regular cash
- **Physical cash stash** (only for very small amounts, and keep it safe)

Never mix emergency savings with fun money or spending accounts. It's meant to stay untouched until you *really* need it.

Tactical Best Practices

- **Label your savings "Emergency Only"** in your app or notebook
- **Set automatic transfers** — even $5/week adds up
- **Visualize the cost of a real emergency** — what would it take to cover it?
- **Don't touch it unless it's urgent** — a sale or craving isn't an emergency

Common Mistakes to Avoid

- Thinking "it won't happen to me" — it always does, eventually
- Dipping into emergency money for non-emergencies
- Waiting until you "have more income" to start saving

- Using credit cards as your only backup — debt can make emergencies worse

Checklist: Build Your Emergency Fund

- ☑ Open or set aside a separate savings account
- ☑ Set a starter goal: $250, then $500
- ☑ Decide on a weekly or monthly savings amount
- ☑ Automate transfers, even if small
- ☑ Track progress and celebrate milestones

Conclusion
Emergencies don't wait for your budget to be ready. That's why building emergency savings — even slowly — is one of the **smartest financial decisions** you can make.

You don't need a huge amount. You just need **a plan and consistency.** Start small, stay focused, and know that when life happens — you've got your own back.

Short-Term vs. Long-Term Savings

When you hear "savings," it might sound like one big category — just money you're not spending right now. But there's actually a big difference between **short-term savings** and **long-term savings** — and knowing that difference helps you stay organized, motivated, and ready for whatever life throws at you.

Think of your savings like a toolbox:
Some tools solve today's problems. Others build your future.

Let's break it down in the simplest way possible.

What Is Short-Term Savings?

Short-term savings is money you set aside for goals you'll need or want to pay for **soon** — usually within the next few weeks or months.

It's money for things that aren't emergencies, but also **aren't part of your everyday budget.** These are things you know are coming.

Common Short-Term Savings Goals:

- Textbooks or school supplies
- A weekend trip with friends
- Holiday gifts
- New phone or headphones
- A concert or event
- Clothing for a new job or internship

🕐 *Timeline:* 1 to 6 months (or sometimes up to 1 year)

💡 *Key Tip:* These are **planned** expenses — not surprises. Saving for them helps you avoid dipping into emergency funds or using credit.

What Is Long-Term Savings?

Long-term savings is money you're setting aside for **much bigger goals** — or to protect your future.

You might not need this money anytime soon, but one day, it could change your life.

Common Long-Term Savings Goals:

- Moving out on your own
- Buying a car
- Paying off student debt early
- Building a bigger emergency fund (3–6 months of expenses)
- Starting a business or going back to school
- Investing or retirement savings (for later in life)

🕐 *Timeline:* 1+ years — often much longer

💡 *Key Tip:* Long-term savings takes **patience.** The sooner you start, the stronger it grows.

Real-World Example: Meet Jordan

What happened:
Jordan is a student working part-time. He saved up $300 for new tires on his car — but then used the same account to buy concert tickets and new clothes.

What went wrong:
Jordan didn't separate his savings goals. He mixed **short-term wants** with **long-term needs**, and ended up short on the money that really mattered.

What we learn:
By separating short-term and long-term savings — even in two labeled folders or digital "buckets" — you can stay focused and avoid spending the wrong money on the wrong thing.

Why the Distinction Matters

When you treat all savings the same, it's easy to:

- Borrow from yourself for fun things
- Lose sight of bigger goals
- Feel like "saving isn't working" because it keeps getting used up

Separating short-term from long-term gives you:

- Clarity — you know what each dollar is for
- Motivation — smaller goals keep you going
- Structure — you're not just saving, you're **saving with purpose**

How to Organize Your Savings

Strategy 1: Use Labeled Savings Buckets

Most banks or apps now let you create multiple savings folders in one account.

Examples:

- "Emergency Fund"
- "Spring Break Trip"
- "Moving Out Fund"
- "Laptop Upgrade"

Strategy 2: Use Two Separate Accounts

Keep long-term savings in a high-yield savings account (or somewhere slightly harder to touch), and short-term in a more accessible one.

Strategy 3: Set Automatic Transfers for Each Goal

Send $5/week to one goal, $10/week to another — and watch both grow.

Tactical Best Practices

- **Set specific goals** for both timeframes: "Save $200 for travel by June" vs. "Save $2,000 to move out in two years"
- **Track each goal separately** — on paper, in an app, or digitally
- **Celebrate reaching short-term goals** — it builds confidence for long-term ones
- **Make long-term savings harder to access** — fewer temptations = more success

Common Mistakes to Avoid

- Mixing all savings into one pile — and losing track of what it's for
- Using long-term savings for quick fun
- Setting no timeline — saving "just because" often loses momentum
- Forgetting to reward yourself when you hit a goal

Checklist: Start Building Both Savings Types

☑ Set one short-term goal (e.g., "Save $150 for new shoes by next month")

☑ Set one long-term goal (e.g., "Save $1,000 to move out next year")

☑ Choose where you'll keep each fund (app folder, separate account, etc.)

☑ Set automatic transfers — even small ones

☑ Track your progress weekly or monthly

Conclusion

Saving money isn't just one goal — it's many goals with different timelines. Short-term savings gives you flexibility and freedom. Long-term savings builds security and opportunity. You don't have to choose — you just need a **plan that separates the two.**

Start small. Stay clear. And give every dollar a job it can be proud of.

AI Reminders and Auto-Savings Features

One of the biggest reasons people struggle to save money or stick to a budget isn't that they don't care — it's that they **forget** or they **don't make it automatic.**

That's where AI-powered tools can make a huge difference. With the help of reminders, nudges, and smart savings features, **you can stay consistent without even thinking about it.**

When AI handles the routine — you're free to focus on your goals.

Let's break down how these features work and how to use them.

What Are AI Reminders?

AI reminders are **smart alerts** that help you stay on top of your money without needing to constantly check your balance or calendar.

Instead of a generic notification like "Pay your bill," AI reminders are based on your habits and patterns. They say things like:

- "You usually overspend on weekends — try to hold back this Friday."
- "You're $25 over your grocery budget this month."
- "You haven't added to savings this week — want to do it now?"

These reminders are:

- **Personalized** to your spending
- **Timely** so they catch you before a mistake
- **Actionable**, with buttons to save, snooze, or review

💡 *Think of AI reminders as your money-savvy friend who always speaks up at the right time.*

What Is Auto-Savings?

Auto-savings is when your budgeting app or bank automatically moves small amounts of money into savings — on a schedule or based on your spending.

It uses AI to:

- Calculate what you can afford to save
- Choose the best time to move money
- Prevent you from overdrafting or over-saving
- Build savings without you having to decide each time

These features remove the **willpower** and **guesswork** — and turn saving into something that happens *on its own*.

Types of Auto-Savings Features (With Examples)

Round-Up Savings

Every time you spend, the app rounds up your purchase and saves the difference.

Example: You buy coffee for $3.40 → app rounds up to $4.00 → saves $0.60.

Great for building savings slowly without noticing.

Scheduled Auto-Saves

You choose a day (e.g., every Friday) and the app moves a fixed amount into your savings.

Example: $10 every payday, or $5 every Sunday.

Great for building consistency.

Smart Auto-Saving Based on Your Spending

Some AI apps watch your cash flow and decide how much you *can* afford to save each week — then do it for you.

Example: Cleo or Digit might say, "You didn't spend much this week — we moved $8.50 into savings for you."

Great for people with inconsistent income.

Goal-Based Auto-Saving

You set a goal (like "Save $300 for textbooks"), and the app figures out how to get there on time — dividing the amount into small, automatic pieces.

Example: "To hit your goal in 3 months, we'll save $25 every 2 weeks."

Real-World Example: Meet Aisha

What happened:
Aisha always *meant* to save, but kept forgetting. She downloaded an app with AI reminders and auto-saving. It started saving $5 here and there — sometimes after coffee runs, sometimes after work.

What changed:
After three months, she had $140 saved — and never felt like she "gave anything up." The AI reminders also helped her avoid overspending on weekends, just by nudging her before she ordered food.

What we learn:
Automation works. Aisha didn't become a budgeting genius overnight — she just set up smart systems that worked quietly in the background.

Tactical Best Practices

- **Set up both round-ups and weekly auto-saves** — a powerful combo
- **Keep reminders turned on** — let your app coach you
- **Name your savings goals** — makes reminders feel more personal
- **Choose low-spending days** for auto-saves — like Mondays or post-payday
- **Review saved amounts monthly** — seeing progress keeps you motivated

Common Mistakes to Avoid

- Ignoring reminders because they feel repetitive — they're based on your behavior
- Turning off auto-saves "until next month" — momentum matters
- Forgetting to label savings goals — you're more likely to dip into "unnamed" money
- Relying only on manual savings — we all forget sometimes

Checklist: Set Up AI-Powered Savings

☑ Choose a budgeting app or bank that supports AI features
☑ Turn on **smart notifications** and allow spending access
☑ Set up **round-up savings** if available
☑ Schedule a small weekly auto-save (e.g., $5)
☑ Create at least one **goal-based savings bucket**
☑ Let the app suggest changes and follow at least one recommendation

Conclusion

AI tools aren't here to control your money — they're here to **support your habits**. With the right reminders and automatic savings features in place, you don't need to be perfect. You just need to be *consistent* — and let the system do the rest.

One decision now can lead to dozens of smart moves later — all made for you.

CHAPTER 5

Smart Spending with AI

How to Spot Wasteful Spending

Ever feel like your money just *disappears*?
Like no matter how much you earn or save, it's gone faster than you expected?

Chances are, you're leaking money through **wasteful spending** — small or unnecessary purchases that don't actually improve your life but silently drain your budget.

The first step to taking control of your money is learning how to **spot what's wasteful** — so you can stop it, fix it, and save more without feeling deprived.

What Is Wasteful Spending?

Wasteful spending is any money spent on things you:

- Didn't plan for
- Don't use or enjoy
- Could've gotten for less
- Didn't even realize you were spending on

It's not about being super strict or never having fun. It's about **not letting money slip away without value.**

The Difference Between *Fun* and *Waste*

Fun Spending (Good)	Wasteful Spending (Bad)
You plan for it	You forget it happened
You enjoy it fully	You regret it later
It fits your budget	It messes up your budget
You'd do it again	You feel guilty afterward

💡 *Not all spending is bad. Wasteful spending is money that gives you little to nothing in return.*

Common Signs of Wasteful Spending

Watch out for these **red flags**:

1. "Where did my money go?"

If you look at your bank account and feel confused or surprised by the balance — there's likely hidden spending going on.

2. Small habits that add up

- Daily coffee runs ($5 x 20 days = $100/month)
- Multiple streaming services you rarely use
- In-game or app purchases that don't last
- Late-night food orders out of boredom

One or two of these are fine. But **repeating them without tracking**? That's waste.

3. Subscription traps

You signed up for a free trial and forgot to cancel.
Or you pay $9.99/month for something you haven't used in weeks.
That's money draining with **zero value.**

4. Impulse buys

If you constantly buy things just because they're on sale, trending, or "might be useful later" — you're spending emotionally, not intentionally.

5. Things you don't use

Check your closet, drawers, or phone apps. How many of those things did you pay for... and never touch again?

Real-World Example: Meet Andre

What happened:
Andre is a student who kept saying he was "broke" — even though he earned $1,200 a month. He wasn't sure where his money was going, until he reviewed his last month of spending.

What went wrong:
He discovered he had spent:

- $135 on fast food
- $48 on random app store purchases
- $72 on two subscriptions he forgot about
- $60 on clothes he hasn't worn yet

Total waste? Over **$300** — in one month.

What we learn:
Andre didn't need more income. He needed more **awareness.** Once he spotted the waste, he was able to cut it in half — and put that extra money toward savings and school supplies.

How to Spot Wasteful Spending in Your Own Budget

1. Review your last 30 days of transactions

Use your bank app, credit card history, or budgeting app. List out every purchase — no matter how small.

2. Highlight anything that:

- You forgot you bought
- You barely used
- You wouldn't buy again
- You bought out of boredom or stress

3. Look for repeat patterns

- "Every Sunday I order food I don't finish"
- "I always overspend when I'm tired or scrolling late at night"
- "I keep buying clothes, but never wear half of them"

This isn't about guilt — it's about **awareness.**

Tactical Best Practices

- **Use a budgeting app** to sort expenses by category and spot outliers
- **Check your subscriptions monthly** — cancel anything you don't use
- **Use the "Would I buy it again?" test** for recent purchases
- **Add a 24-hour pause rule** before buying anything over $20
- **Only shop from a list** — whether groceries or online items

Common Mistakes to Avoid

- Thinking "It's just a few dollars" — small leaks sink big ships
- Blaming income when the issue is spending habits
- Avoiding transaction reviews because they're "boring" — they're the map to your money
- Justifying every purchase as "self-care" — real self-care includes **financial peace**

Checklist: Identify and Eliminate Waste

- [x] Review your past month's transactions
- [x] Highlight anything you forgot about or regret
- [x] Add up how much of it was *truly wasted*
- [x] Choose 1–2 habits to reduce next month
- [x] Redirect those dollars to savings or a goal you care about

Conclusion

Wasteful spending isn't about what other people think — it's about **your own values**. If you're spending on things you don't use, don't enjoy, or don't remember — that's money working against you.

Spotting waste doesn't mean cutting out joy. It means cutting out the stuff that adds nothing, so you have *more* for what really matters.

Price Comparison Made Simple

Every time you spend money — whether it's on food, clothes, tech, or school supplies — you're making a choice. And if you're not comparing prices, **you could be overpaying without even knowing it.**

Price comparison is one of the fastest, easiest ways to save money — without giving anything up.

It doesn't mean being cheap or spending hours searching. It means being smart, patient, and learning how to make the **best deal your default.**

Let's break it down.

What Is Price Comparison?

Price comparison means checking different options before you buy something, so you don't pay more than you have to for the exact same thing.

It's about asking:

- Is there a cheaper version of this somewhere else?
- Can I get the same quality for less?
- Do I really need the brand-name version?
- Is this price fair — or inflated?

You don't need to hunt for hours. Often, **60 seconds** is enough to spot a better deal.

Why It Matters (Especially for Students)

- You're working with a **limited budget**
- Small price differences **add up fast**
- Stores and apps often change prices daily
- Many people overpay out of habit or convenience

Once you build the price-check habit, saving $5, $10, or even $50 becomes normal — and that adds up to serious savings over time.

Real-World Example: Meet Elena

What happened:
Elena needed a new pair of headphones. She almost bought a pair for $80 at the campus tech store, but decided to check online first.

What changed:
She found the exact same model for $59 on a major retailer's website — with free shipping and a coupon. Total savings: **$21** for 2 minutes of searching.

What we learn:
One small habit change = real money saved. That $21 went into her savings goal for a weekend trip.

Where to Compare Prices

In-Store vs. Online

- Check Amazon, Walmart, Target, or Best Buy before buying in-store
- Use **barcode scanner apps** (like ShopSavvy or Google Lens) to instantly compare

Online Tools and Extensions

- **Honey** or **Capital One Shopping** browser extensions automatically search for better prices or coupon codes
- **Google Shopping** lets you compare multiple retailers in one search

Mobile Shopping Apps

- Use price comparison tools inside apps like Flip, Rakuten, or even the store's own app
- Check price histories on sites like **CamelCamelCamel** (for Amazon)

💡 Bonus Tip: Ask for a Price Match

Many retailers will match a lower price from a competitor if you show them proof.

What to Compare (and When)

You don't need to compare prices on *everything*. Focus on:

Good for Comparing	Less Critical
Tech + electronics	Basic groceries
School supplies	Public transport fares
Books or textbooks	Small snacks or drinks
Clothes + shoes	One-time campus fees
Subscriptions	Emergency services

💡 *General Rule:* Compare anything over **$20** or anything you buy **regularly.**

Tactical Best Practices

- **Always check 2+ places** before buying — even just Google + Amazon
- **Compare total cost** (with shipping, tax, and time)
- **Set price alerts** on tools like Honey or CamelCamelCamel
- **Buy in bulk when it saves you more long term** (e.g., toiletries, pens, snacks)
- **Wait for sales if it's not urgent** — use wishlists to track

Common Mistakes to Avoid

- Assuming the first price you see is the best
- Thinking price = quality (it doesn't always)
- Ignoring shipping or tax when comparing
- Not checking student discounts (many retailers offer them!)
- Forgetting to look for coupons — they're often automatic now with extensions

Checklist: Compare Before You Spend

- ☑ Search for the item on two or more sites
- ☑ Look at total cost (item + shipping + tax)
- ☑ See if a student discount is available
- ☑ Ask about a price match (if shopping in-store)
- ☑ Use a browser extension for coupons or alerts
- ☑ Only buy once you know you're getting a solid deal

Conclusion

Price comparison doesn't make you cheap — it makes you **smart.** Every time you check before you spend, you're protecting your money, making better choices, and building habits that will pay off for life.

It takes less time than you think — and saves more money than you expect.

Budget Alerts on Your Phone

You're busy. You've got school, work, social life — and trying to remember your budget on top of that? Nearly impossible. That's why setting up **budget alerts on your phone** is a game-changer.

Budget alerts act like a digital safety net — catching mistakes before they happen and keeping you in control without constant effort.

They're fast, smart, and work in the background. Let's explore how they work and how to set them up the right way.

What Are Budget Alerts?

Budget alerts are instant notifications sent to your phone when your spending hits certain limits, patterns, or problems.

They help you:

- Know when you're close to overspending
- Track specific categories (like food or transport)
- Avoid surprises in your account
- Stick to your plan *without needing to check constantly*

Think of them as your **budget bodyguards** — giving you real-time updates and reminders so you can make smart choices before things go off track.

Types of Budget Alerts (and How They Help)

Spending Limit Alerts

- You set a max for categories like food, fun, or transport.
- When you get close (e.g., 80%) or go over, your phone pings you.

💡 *Example:* "You've spent $120 of your $150 food budget this month."

Low Balance Alerts

- Get notified when your bank account drops below a certain amount.
- Prevents overdraft fees or missed payments.

💡 *Example:* "Your checking account balance is below $50."

Upcoming Bill Reminders

- Never forget a phone bill, subscription, or rent payment again.
- Some apps link to your accounts and spot bills automatically.

💡 *Example:* "Your phone bill of $65 is due in 3 days."

Unusual Spending Alerts

- AI-powered apps notice if you're spending way more than usual in a category or store.
- Helps you catch impulse buying or emotional spending patterns.

💡 *Example:* "You've spent 40% more on takeout this week than last week."

Goal Progress Alerts

- Reminds you to save toward specific goals — or celebrates when you hit milestones.
- Great for motivation and consistency.

💡 *Example:* "You're halfway to your emergency fund goal!"

Real-World Example: Meet Tyler

What happened:
Tyler wanted to stick to a $100/month fun budget. He set up alerts on his budgeting app. After a few weeks, he got a ping: "You've spent 90% of your fun budget." It stopped him from buying concert tickets he didn't *really* want.

What changed:
Without the alert, Tyler wouldn't have noticed how fast he was spending. He started checking in more often and made his budget last all month — with zero stress.

How to Set Up Budget Alerts (Step-by-Step)

Option 1: Use Your Bank App

Most modern bank apps let you:

- Set low balance alerts
- Turn on bill due notifications
- Get alerts for large transactions

✅ Go to app settings → Notifications → Turn on relevant alerts

Option 2: Use a Budgeting App (with AI)

Apps like:

- **Cleo**
- **Rocket Money**
- **YNAB (You Need a Budget)**
- **Monarch Money**
- **Simplifi by Quicken**

These tools offer personalized, smart alerts based on **your actual habits**, not just basic rules.

☑ Link your accounts → Set budgets for categories → Turn on custom notifications

Option 3: Use Text-Based Money Assistants

Apps like **Cleo** even let you chat with an AI assistant and ask:

- "How much have I spent on food this month?"
- "What's left in my budget?"
- "Warn me if I overspend on coffee again."

You can get alerts through push notifications, texts, or even emails — whatever works best for your style.

Tactical Best Practices

- **Start with 2–3 key alerts** — don't overwhelm yourself
- **Focus on categories where you overspend most** (like food, fun, or subscriptions)
- **Schedule a weekly money check-in** to review alerts
- **Avoid alert fatigue** — turn off what you don't need or respond to

Common Mistakes to Avoid

- Ignoring alerts because "they're just notifications" — take them seriously
- Setting limits too low and getting constant pings — be realistic
- Only using alerts without reviewing your full budget monthly
- Not acting when you get a warning — alerts help, but you have to respond

Checklist: Set Up Your First Budget Alerts

- ☑ Choose a budgeting or banking app with smart notifications
- ☑ Set spending limits for your top 2-3 categories
- ☑ Turn on low balance and bill reminders
- ☑ Customize when and how you receive alerts (push, email, text)
- ☑ Test them for 1 month and adjust as needed

Conclusion

Budget alerts are like guardrails for your money — they don't restrict you, they **protect you**. With just a few taps, you can stop overspending, avoid surprises, and stay on track with almost zero extra effort.

In a world full of distractions, these alerts help you stay focused — and in control.

How AI Shows You Cheaper Choices

One of the easiest ways to save money is also one of the most overlooked:
Choosing the same thing — for less.

And thanks to Artificial Intelligence (AI), you don't have to manually search for deals, compare products, or look up prices every time you shop. Smart AI tools now do the hard work for you — showing you **cheaper options** the moment you're about to spend.

AI doesn't just track your budget — it helps you make **better choices before you spend a dime.**

Let's explore how it works, why it's powerful, and how to use it right.

What Does "Cheaper Choices" Really Mean?

It's not just about buying the **cheapest** thing. It's about getting the **same value** for **less money.**

AI helps you:

- Find the best price for what you already plan to buy
- Spot duplicate or similar items at lower cost
- Catch hidden savings like coupons, discounts, or bundles
- Recommend budget-friendly alternatives based on your spending style

💡 *It's not about spending less — it's about spending smarter.*

How AI Finds Cheaper Options (Step-by-Step)

1. It Watches What You Search or Spend

When you shop online or through certain apps, AI notices what you're looking at or about to buy.

2. It Scans Other Sellers Instantly

AI tools compare thousands of prices, in real time, across other stores or platforms.

3. It Suggests Better Deals

If it finds the same item for less — or a nearly identical version — it pops up with a suggestion:

- "Save $12 by buying from this store instead"
- "This alternative is 30% cheaper and has similar reviews"
- "There's a coupon available — apply it now?"

You don't have to hunt. **The savings come to you.**

Real-World Example: Meet Marcus

What happened:
Marcus was about to buy a $45 USB microphone for class presentations. Right before he clicked "Buy," his AI shopping assistant suggested a similar mic — same features, same rating — for $29 from another seller.

What changed:
He saved **$16 instantly** — no extra effort, no hours of comparing reviews. Just a smarter decision made possible by AI.

What we learn:
The key to smarter spending isn't always saying *no* — it's letting AI show you the **better yes**.

Popular AI Tools That Show Cheaper Choices

Tool	What It Does
Honey	Finds lower prices and coupon codes at checkout
Capital One Shopping	Compares prices across major sites while you shop
Google Shopping	Uses AI to show lowest offers from hundreds of sellers
Cleo	Alerts you to smarter purchases if your spending is getting too high
Rakuten	Finds cash-back deals and cheaper bundles across categories
Amazon Assistant	Compares similar products as you browse

♀ *Most are free and work in your browser or phone.*

What to Use It For

These tools work best for:

- Tech and electronics
- Clothing or shoes
- Household supplies
- School gear and textbooks
- Subscriptions and software
- Personal care products

💡 *Even saving $3–$5 per item adds up fast when you're a student or budgeting monthly.*

Tactical Best Practices

- **Install a browser extension** like Honey or Capital One Shopping — they work automatically
- **Use wishlists** — let the app track price drops and suggest cheaper options later
- **Always check suggested alternatives** — don't default to the first result you see
- **Check the total cost** (including shipping and taxes) — not just the sticker price
- **Stay flexible** — you don't always need the exact brand or color

Common Mistakes to Avoid

- Assuming "top result" = best price (it often isn't)
- Ignoring AI suggestions because "it's only a few dollars"
- Buying name-brand just out of habit
- Forgetting to compare subscriptions or digital services — lots of free or lower-cost versions exist
- Turning off browser alerts because they're "annoying" — those alerts are **saving you money**

Checklist: Use AI to Find Better Deals

- ☑ Install a trusted AI shopping extension or app
- ☑ Try comparing one product across 2–3 platforms before buying
- ☑ Let AI notify you of coupons or cheaper sellers
- ☑ Reconsider brand-name purchases if there's a better-value option
- ☑ Track what you save in a note or budget app — to stay motivated

Conclusion

AI makes finding cheaper choices faster, smarter, and automatic. You don't have to change what you want — you just get it **for less.** In a world where prices rise fast, your money needs to work smarter. AI makes that possible.

The next time you're about to buy something, pause for 5 seconds — and let AI do the work. It could save you $5... or $50.

CHAPTER 6

Reaching Your Goals

What a Financial Goal Looks Like (Examples)

Budgeting without a goal is like driving with no destination — you burn fuel, but you don't go anywhere meaningful.

That's why setting **financial goals** is one of the smartest moves you can make, especially as a beginner. It turns your money from something you just **spend** into something you can **build with.**

A financial goal is simply a **money target** — something specific you want to achieve, afford, or prepare for.

Let's break it down clearly, with examples you can actually use.

What Is a Financial Goal?

A **financial goal** is something you're saving or budgeting toward on purpose — not by accident, not "if there's money left."

A good goal is:

- Clear (you know what it's for)
- Specific (you know the amount)
- Realistic (you can reach it with your income)
- Timed (you know when you want to hit it)

It's not just "I want to save more."
It's:
"I want to save $300 for a new phone by December."

Why Goals Matter

- They give your money direction and purpose
- They make budgeting feel **motivating**, not limiting
- They help you say "no" to things that don't move you forward
- They track your progress — so you can celebrate wins

Without a goal, saving can feel boring or pointless. With a goal, every dollar feels like a step forward.

Real-World Example: Meet Sara

What happened:
Sara used to spend whatever she had. Then she set a goal to buy a used laptop for school — $450 total. She saved $30 a week for 4 months, skipped a few takeout meals, and made it happen *before* the semester started.

What changed:
The goal gave her motivation. She wasn't just "spending less" — she was building something. And when she hit it, she felt **proud, not restricted.**

Examples of Student-Friendly Financial Goals

Here are some real, reachable financial goals — categorized by time and purpose.

Short-Term Goals (1–3 Months)

Goal	Amount	Why It Matters
Save $100 for holiday gifts	$100	Avoids last-minute panic or debt
Build a $250 emergency fund	$250	Gives you peace of mind
Buy a basic printer for class	$60–$100	Helps you avoid late-night print shops
Save $75 for a school event or trip	$75	You can say "yes" without stress
Save $20/week to upgrade headphones	$80/month	Turns small habits into real results

Medium-Term Goals (3–12 Months)

Goal	Amount	Why It Matters
Save $600 for spring break travel	$600	Prepares you early and stress-free
Build a $500 emergency fund	$500	Covers surprise expenses like repairs
Buy a refurbished laptop	$400–$800	An essential tool for school or work
Pay off $300 in credit card debt	$300	Frees up future income and improves credit
Save $1,000 to move out	$1,000	Gets you ready for independence

Long-Term Goals (1 Year or More)

Goal	Amount	Why It Matters
Save $2,500 for a car down payment	$2,500	Helps you avoid bad financing deals
Pay off a student loan chunk early	$1,000+	Cuts down interest over time
Build a $1,500–$2,000 emergency fund	$1,500+	Covers 1–2 months of expenses
Save for grad school or certification	Varies	Expands your future opportunities
Start a small business or side hustle	$500–$3,000	Turns ideas into income

How to Set a Financial Goal (Step-by-Step)

1. **Pick something real you care about**
   → New phone? Travel? Emergency fund?
2. **Decide the total amount needed**
   → Research the actual cost, don't guess.
3. **Set a timeline**
   → Example: 3 months, 6 months, 1 year
4. **Break it down into small steps**
   → $300 in 3 months = $25/week
5. **Track your progress**
   → Use an app, spreadsheet, or paper tracker
   → Celebrate when you hit milestones!

Tactical Best Practices

- **Start with one small goal** — build momentum
- **Automate your savings** — let apps move small amounts weekly
- **Tie your goal to a real date** — like a holiday, semester, or event
- **Keep a reminder visible** — a phone wallpaper, sticky note, or app alert
- **Use goals to say "no" to impulse buys** — "That's not in line with my goal right now."

Common Mistakes to Avoid

- Setting vague goals like "save more money" — no amount, no date
- Choosing unrealistic targets (like $1,000 in 1 month on a $500 income)
- Forgetting to track progress — then losing motivation
- Not adjusting the goal if your income or timeline changes
- Mixing up savings for fun with savings for emergencies — separate them

Checklist: Set Your First Real Financial Goal

- [x] Choose a specific thing you want to save for
- [x] Write down the total cost
- [x] Set a deadline (date or month)
- [x] Break it into weekly or monthly steps
- [x] Track your progress in a place you'll see it

Conclusion

Financial goals turn saving from a chore into a **mission.** They keep you focused, motivated, and clear on what matters to *you* — not just what others say you should spend on.

Whether it's $50 or $5,000, your goal is valid. Make it real, break it down, and watch your money work for something that matters.

Step-by-Step Goal Planning

You've got a goal — now what?
Knowing *what* you want is important, but knowing *how* to actually reach it is what makes the difference.

Step-by-step goal planning turns big dreams into small, doable actions.**
It breaks your money target into simple steps so you stay focused, motivated, and on track — even if you're starting small.

This is where your savings become real.

Why Planning Your Goal Matters

Anyone can *wish* for something — a trip, a new laptop, a safety cushion of emergency money.
But goals without a plan lead to:

- Delays
- Frustration
- Giving up

When you follow a step-by-step plan, your goal stops being overwhelming and starts being achievable.

The 5-Step Process for Goal Planning

✅ Step 1: Pick One Clear Goal

What do you want to save for?

Make it specific.
Bad: "Save some money"
Good: "Save $300 for a used iPad by December 1st"

📌 *Tip:* If you're new to saving, start with a **short-term goal** under $500 — so you can win early and build confidence.

✅ Step 2: Find Out How Much It Costs

Know the **real price**, not just a guess.

Search online, get a quote, or ask around. Don't just assume it's "probably like $100."
You can't hit a target if you don't know the number.

📌 *Tip:* Add tax, shipping, or extra fees to your total to avoid surprises.

✅ Step 3: Set a Realistic Deadline

When do you want to hit this goal?

Short-term = 1–3 months
Medium-term = 3–12 months
Long-term = 1+ year

Example: "I want to save $300 in 3 months — by December 1st."

📌 *Tip:* Tie your deadline to something real (semester start, birthday, trip date) to stay motivated.

☑ Step 4: Break It Down Into Smaller Pieces

Divide your goal by the time you have.

Use this formula:
Total amount ÷ Number of weeks = Weekly savings goal

Example:
$300 goal ÷ 12 weeks = **$25 per week**

This tells you *exactly* what to do. No guessing.

📌 *Tip:* You can also break it into **daily** amounts if weekly feels too big.
$300 ÷ 90 days = **$3.33 per day**

☑ Step 5: Track and Adjust Weekly

Make your progress visible.

Use a:

- Notebook
- Free budgeting app
- Google Sheet
- Savings tracker printable
- Visual chart or sticky note on your wall

Review it once a week:

- Did you save what you planned?
- Are you ahead or behind?
- Do you need to adjust the amount or deadline?

📌 *Tip:* Celebrate small wins. Every $10 saved is a step closer to your goal.

Real-World Example: Meet Devin

Goal: Save $240 for a weekend trip in 8 weeks
Step-by-step plan:

1. Checked bus fare, hotel, and food: $240 total
2. Set deadline: Trip is in 2 months
3. $240 ÷ 8 weeks = $30/week
4. Set a weekly auto-transfer for $30
5. Tracked progress using a simple savings tracker on his wall

Result: Devin hit his goal *2 weeks early* and had extra spending money — no stress, no credit card debt.

Tactical Best Practices

- **Round up your weekly savings** by $1–2 for cushion
- **Use calendar reminders** to check in on your goal every Sunday or payday
- **Automate your weekly transfer** if possible — avoid temptation
- **Name your savings account** after your goal (e.g., "Trip Fund" or "New Laptop")
- **Use apps like Cleo, YNAB, or Qapital** to track visually and build habits

Common Mistakes to Avoid

- Skipping the math — vague goals are easy to quit
- Not tracking weekly — you'll lose momentum
- Setting unrealistic deadlines (e.g., $500 in 2 weeks with a $300 income)
- Mixing goal savings with spending money
- Giving up after one missed week — adjust and keep going!

Checklist: Plan Your Next Financial Goal

- ☑ Choose one specific goal you care about
- ☑ Find the total amount you need — be exact
- ☑ Pick a target date
- ☑ Divide into weekly savings goals
- ☑ Set a tracking method (app, chart, or journal)
- ☑ Start saving — and adjust as needed

Conclusion

A financial goal without a plan is just a wish. But when you break it down into weekly steps, everything becomes clearer — and more possible. You don't need to save it all at once. You just need to **start, stick with it, and adjust as you go.**

Every dollar saved brings you closer — one step at a time.

How to Avoid Quitting Halfway

Starting is exciting. You set a budget. You make a plan. You're ready to save money and hit your goals.

But then life happens. You overspend one week. A friend invites you out. You skip tracking for a few days. Suddenly, you feel off-track — and it's tempting to give up altogether.

Most people don't fail because the goal was too big — they quit halfway because they didn't have a system for staying on track.

Let's fix that. Here's how to stay in the game, even when motivation fades.

Why People Quit Midway

Before we look at the solution, let's understand the **real reasons** people stop budgeting or saving:

- **Progress feels slow**
- **One mistake makes them feel like they "failed"**
- **They never built reminders or habits**
- **They dip into savings for other stuff**
- **The goal wasn't personal enough**

Good news: Every one of these can be solved with simple strategies.

7 Real Ways to Stay Committed

✅ 1. Make Your Goal Visible — Every Day

Put your savings tracker on your wall. Rename your bank account "Emergency Fund" or "New Laptop." Keep a sticky note on your mirror.

📌 *Out of sight = out of mind. Put your goal where you'll see it every day.*

✅ 2. Use "Pause" — Don't Quit

Life happens. If you miss a week or overspend, **don't delete your plan — just pause it.**
Pick it up again next week.
Being consistent > being perfect.

📌 *One mistake doesn't undo weeks of progress — unless you let it.*

✅ 3. Automate What You Can

Auto-transfer your weekly savings. Set budget alerts. Use reminder apps.
Remove "remembering" from the equation.

📌 *Discipline is hard. Automation is easy.*

✅ 4. Track Progress in Small Chunks

If your goal is $500, break it into ten $50 milestones.
Checking off a mini-win every week keeps you motivated.

📌 *Progress feels real when you can see it.*

✅ 5. Build in Rewards Along the Way

Every time you hit a milestone, celebrate — without blowing your budget.
For example:

- Hit $100 saved? Treat yourself to a $5 dessert.
- 4 weeks of perfect tracking? Take a night off from cooking.

📌 *Rewards train your brain to associate budgeting with success.*

✅ 6. Tell Someone You Trust

Let a friend or sibling know your goal. Or post it anonymously in a budgeting community.
When you say it out loud, you feel more accountable.

📌 *Quiet goals are easy to quit. Shared goals stick longer.*

✅ 7. Remind Yourself *Why* You Started

Write it down and read it weekly:

- "So I don't have to borrow money again."
- "So I can finally afford that weekend trip."
- "So I feel in control of my life."

📌 *When the reason is strong, the excuses feel weak.*

Real-World Example: Meet Leo

What happened:
Leo set a goal to save $600 in 3 months for a new phone. At week 5, he dipped into his fund for fast food and felt like he had "ruined it."

What changed:
Instead of quitting, he paused for 2 weeks, adjusted his weekly goal slightly, and picked up again. He hit the full $600 in week 14 instead of week 12 — and still got his phone without using a credit card.

What we learn:
One wrong step doesn't end the journey. Leo kept going because he focused on progress, not perfection.

Tactical Best Practices

- **Schedule a 10-minute weekly money check-in** (same day, every week)
- **Keep a one-line journal**: "This week, I saved $___ toward ___."
- **Reset your goal timeline** if needed — life changes, and that's okay
- **Create a goal mantra** and repeat it: *"I'm learning. I'm building. I'm growing."*
- **If you're tempted to quit, ask yourself: Would Future Me be glad I stopped today?**

Common Mistakes to Avoid

- Thinking a missed week = total failure
- Hiding from your numbers when things get tough
- Comparing yourself to others instead of your past self
- Setting goals that are too big, too fast
- Forgetting why you started in the first place

Checklist: Stay on Track and Avoid Quitting

- [x] Make your goal visible (tracker, sticky note, phone background)
- [x] Break big goals into small steps
- [x] Automate savings if possible
- [x] Set a weekly budget check-in time
- [x] Build in mini rewards
- [x] Talk to someone about your goal
- [x] Be kind to yourself — progress beats perfection

Conclusion

Budgeting isn't a sprint. It's a new habit — and every habit takes time. What matters most isn't being perfect — it's **staying in the game.** When you feel like quitting, pause, breathe, and come back to your "why." You'll be surprised how far you can go if you just don't stop.

AI Helping Track Progress Like a Coach

Imagine having a personal finance coach who never forgets, never judges, and always keeps you on track. That's what AI can be — a smart, quiet coach that follows your progress, celebrates your wins, and gives you reminders exactly when you need them.

AI doesn't just help you make a budget — it helps you **stick to it** by tracking your progress automatically.

And it's not about being perfect. It's about having a system that helps you move forward, **even when you're busy, tired, or tempted to quit**.

How AI Works Like a Personal Money Coach

Here's what a real financial coach would do:

- Check in regularly
- Tell you if you're off-track
- Motivate you when you're doing well
- Help you make adjustments when life changes

That's exactly what today's AI-powered apps can do — but automatically, and for free (or cheap).

What AI Can Track for You

AI Tracking Feature	What It Helps With
Weekly spending summaries	Keeps you aware of where your money's going
Budget alerts	Warns you before you go over
Goal progress meters	Shows you how close you are to reaching your savings target
Personalized tips	Gives you smarter options based on your habits
Pattern detection	Notices when your spending shifts (good or bad)

📌 *All this happens behind the scenes — no spreadsheets or math required.*

Real-World Example: Meet Naomi

What happened:
Naomi set a goal to save $400 in 10 weeks for a new tablet. She used a budgeting app with AI tracking. Each week, it told her:

- How much she saved
- How close she was to her goal
- If she was ahead or behind
- How to adjust if she missed a week

What changed:
Naomi didn't have to guess or stress. The AI coach kept her steady. She hit her $400 goal **one week early** — and gained confidence to start planning a new goal.

Best AI Tools That Act Like a Coach

These apps use smart reminders, visual trackers, and personalized feedback to help you stick with your plan:

Tool	What It Does
Cleo	Chats with you about your spending and goals, uses humor + reminders
You Need A Budget (YNAB)	Gives progress bars, goal tracking, and habit coaching
Monarch Money	Tracks multiple goals, budgets, and gives real-time updates
Digit (now part of Oportun)	Moves money automatically and shows progress per goal
Qapital	Lets you create custom savings rules and goals, tracks all progress visually

📌 *Many of these tools send updates by text or notification — just like a coach checking in with you.*

How to Use AI to Stay On Track (Step-by-Step)

✅ **Step 1: Choose Your Tool**

Pick one app that feels easy and clear. You don't need five — just one you'll use.

✅ **Step 2: Set a Clear Goal in the App**

E.g., "Save $300 for a bike by June 30"
The app will set up a progress bar or weekly schedule.

☑ Step 3: Turn On Notifications

Let the AI remind you when you:

- Hit milestones
- Miss a deposit
- Have money left to save this week

☑ Step 4: Review Weekly Updates

Every Sunday (or payday), check your progress:

- How much have you saved?
- Are you on track?
- What needs to change?

☑ Step 5: Let It Coach You

If the app suggests adjusting your plan or celebrates your progress — take the advice. It's using your real data to help you succeed.

Tactical Best Practices

- **Always keep goal notifications turned on** — they're your progress checkpoints
- **Let the AI adjust your savings if income changes** (many apps do this)
- **Use visual trackers** — progress bars keep your brain engaged
- **Use reminders to do weekly reviews** — 5 minutes max
- **If your app has chat-based coaching (like Cleo), use it for motivation**

Common Mistakes to Avoid

- Turning off alerts because "they're annoying" — they're your progress compass
- Ignoring AI tips or suggested adjustments
- Trying to track everything in your head — that's what the tool is for
- Giving up if one week goes badly — AI will help you recover
- Using too many apps and getting overwhelmed — keep it simple

Checklist: Use AI as Your Progress Partner

- ☑ Choose one app with strong goal-tracking features
- ☑ Set a realistic financial goal with a timeline
- ☑ Turn on reminders and notifications
- ☑ Check progress weekly
- ☑ Follow suggestions and let the AI coach you
- ☑ Celebrate when you hit milestones

Conclusion

AI isn't just a tool — it's a teammate. It helps you stay consistent, track your growth, and recover faster when life throws a curveball. With a smart system in place, your goals don't get forgotten. They stay alive, visible, and achievable.

It's like having a coach in your pocket — guiding you quietly, every step of the way.

CHAPTER 7

Debt Explained Simply

H2: What Debt Means in Easy Words

Let's make this simple:

Debt is money you **borrow** — and have to **pay back later**, usually **with extra fees**.

If you've ever borrowed $20 from a friend and promised to pay it back next week, you've had **a tiny form of debt**. But when it comes to credit cards, loans, or payment plans, debt can get **bigger, longer, and more expensive** if you're not careful.

So, let's break it down clearly — what debt is, how it works, and what it means for your money.

The Basic Idea of Debt

You borrow money now → You use it → You **owe** that money back → Often with **interest** added on top.

Debt can come from:

- Credit cards
- Student loans
- Car loans
- "Buy now, pay later" plans (like Klarna, Afterpay, etc.)
- Borrowing from a friend or family member

📌 *If you use someone else's money today, and promise to return it later — that's debt.*

Why People Go Into Debt

- They don't have enough saved for something they need
- They want to buy something now and pay for it later
- They believe they'll have the money "soon"
- They didn't plan ahead — or had an emergency

💡 **Debt can be helpful or harmful — depending on how you use it.**

The Two Parts of Debt You Must Understand

1. Principal = the amount you borrow

Example: You borrow $500 → that's your **principal**

2. Interest = the extra fee you pay for borrowing

Example: The lender charges 10% → You owe **$500 + $50 = $550**

📌 *Interest is how the bank or lender makes money from you.*

Real-World Example: Meet Jordan

What happened:
Jordan wanted a $600 gaming console but didn't have the money. A store offered "Buy now, pay later" — four monthly payments of $150.

What went wrong:
Jordan missed two payments and got hit with late fees. In the end, he paid **$680** for a $600 console — and it hurt his credit.

What we learn:
Debt seems easy at first — but it **costs more later** if you don't stay on top of it.

Common Types of Debt (Explained Simply)

Type of Debt	What It Is	How It Works
Credit Card	You borrow up to a limit, repay monthly	If unpaid, interest builds fast (15%–30%!)
Student Loan	Borrowed money for school	Must repay after graduation — with interest
Personal Loan	Borrowed lump sum for big expenses	Fixed monthly payments, interest varies
"Buy Now, Pay Later"	Split payments over weeks or months	Often no interest — but late fees if you miss
Car Loan	Borrowed money to buy a vehicle	Monthly payments with interest until fully paid

How Debt Affects Your Life

☑ **If managed well:**

- Helps you build credit
- Lets you pay for big things over time
- Can be part of your financial plan

If mismanaged:

- Costs more than you expected
- Hurts your credit score
- Traps you in a cycle of always owing money
- Adds stress to your life

📌 *Debt isn't always bad — but it's always serious.*

Tactical Best Practices

- **Only borrow what you can repay on time**
- **Always know the due date** for any loan or credit payment
- **Avoid minimum payments** — they keep you in debt longer
- **Plan for interest** — it's part of the total cost
- **Don't borrow for wants** — save up instead

Common Mistakes to Avoid

- Thinking of credit as "free money" — it's not
- Ignoring the total cost (including interest or fees)
- Using debt to buy non-essential things
- Missing payments — it hurts your credit and adds fees
- Borrowing more just because you "got approved"

Checklist: Understanding Debt Before You Borrow

- ☑ Know how much you're borrowing (the principal)
- ☑ Understand the interest rate or fees
- ☑ Check the repayment timeline
- ☑ Set reminders so you never miss payments
- ☑ Ask yourself: "Can I afford to repay this *on time*?"
- ☑ Ask one more question: "Is this a **need** or a **want**?"

Conclusion

Debt is not evil — but it is powerful. It lets you borrow money when you need it. But if you don't manage it carefully, it can quietly take control of your money — and your peace of mind.

Know the facts. Ask the right questions. Borrow only when it helps, not when it hurts.

Good Debt vs. Bad Debt

Not all debt is bad. In fact, some types of debt can **help you grow**, **build credit**, or **create future opportunities** — if you use them wisely.

But there's also debt that drains your money, adds stress, and keeps you stuck. That's what we call **bad debt**.

The key isn't to fear debt — it's to **understand the difference** between good debt and bad debt, and make smart choices with both.

Let's break it down in simple terms.

What Is Good Debt?

Good debt helps you:

- Build something valuable
- Grow your income or future options
- Improve your long-term life
- Usually has **low interest** and a clear purpose

It's a **tool**, not a trap.

✓ Examples of Good Debt:

Type	Why It Can Be Good
Student loans	Education can lead to higher income later
Affordable car loan	Reliable transport can help you get or keep a job
Small business loan	Lets you build something that earns money
Low-interest personal loan for emergencies	Avoids worse problems like eviction or medical risk

📌 Good debt is **planned, managed,** and **used for something that helps you grow.**

What Is Bad Debt?

Bad debt is when you borrow:

- For things that lose value fast
- To buy things you don't really need
- With **high interest** or unclear repayment plans
- Without a strategy to pay it off

It's often emotional, rushed, or based on short-term thinking.

Examples of Bad Debt:

Type	Why It's Risky
High-interest credit card balances	Interest piles up quickly if not paid monthly
"Buy now, pay later" for clothes or gadgets	Looks easy, but adds up fast with fees and missed payments
Payday loans	Extremely high fees and traps people in cycles of debt
Borrowing for non-essential stuff (concerts, takeout, fashion)	You enjoy the moment, but owe for weeks or months after

🏷️ *Bad debt takes your money — and gives you very little back.*

Real-World Example: Meet Ava and Liam

Ava's Choice – Good Debt:
Ava took out a **small student loan** to pay for a certification program. She finished in 6 months and now earns $350 more per month. Her debt is going down, and her income went up.

Liam's Choice – Bad Debt:
Liam got a new credit card and used it to buy $500 worth of clothes and takeout. He didn't pay it off on time, and now owes $630 with interest. He regrets the purchases but still has to pay them off.

What we learn:
Debt used for long-term value **can pay off**. Debt used for short-term wants **sticks around longer than the joy.**

5 Questions to Ask Before Taking on Debt

1. **Does this help me grow or earn more later?**
2. **Can I afford to repay it — on time?**
3. **Is there a cheaper way to get this?**
4. **Is this a need or a want?**
5. **What's the total cost after interest and fees?**

If you can't answer clearly, pause. Don't rush into borrowing.

Tactical Best Practices

- Use debt only when it adds **long-term value** (like education, transport, or emergency needs)
- Choose **low-interest loans** whenever possible
- Have a **repayment plan** *before* you borrow
- Pay off credit card balances **in full** every month
- Avoid debt for non-essentials — save up instead
- Use apps to calculate the **true cost** of any loan or payment plan

Common Mistakes to Avoid

- Using credit cards for emotional spending
- Thinking "if I qualify for a loan, I must need it" — you don't
- Borrowing without a plan to repay
- Ignoring interest rates — even 1% can make a big difference
- Confusing **wants** with **needs** when making debt decisions

Good Debt vs. Bad Debt (At a Glance)

Good Debt	Bad Debt
Has a purpose that improves your future	Buys things that lose value quickly
Often low interest	Usually high interest or fees
You have a repayment plan	No clear way to pay it back
Leads to more opportunities (job, skills, business)	Creates stress, regret, and ongoing bills
Helps build positive credit history	Can destroy your credit if unmanaged

Checklist: Decide If a Debt Is Worth It

- ✓ Will this improve my life long-term?
- ✓ Do I understand the total cost — interest, fees, timeline?
- ✓ Is this debt cheaper than other options?
- ✓ Can I pay it off comfortably, even if things go wrong?
- ✓ Is this part of a bigger plan (school, job, stability)?
- ✓ If I wait and save, could I avoid this debt entirely?

Conclusion
Debt isn't automatically bad. What matters is **how you use it, why you use it, and whether you can manage it well.**
Good debt can build your future. Bad debt can break your budget. The difference is in your decision-making.

Know the facts, ask the right questions, and **only take on debt when it helps you move forward.**

Why Credit Cards Can Be Tricky

Credit cards can feel like magic:
Swipe → You get what you want → Pay later.

But that "pay later" part? That's where things get complicated — and sometimes expensive.

Credit cards aren't free money. They're a short-term loan with long-term consequences if you're not careful.

Used the right way, a credit card can build your credit and help you in emergencies. Used the wrong way, it can quietly pile up debt, interest, and stress. Let's break it down in plain English.

What Is a Credit Card, Really?

A **credit card** lets you **borrow money from a bank** to make purchases. You don't pay right away — you pay it back **later**, usually once a month.

Every card has a **credit limit** (how much you're allowed to borrow), and if you don't pay it all back each month, the bank charges **interest** on the leftover balance.

📌 *In simple terms: it's a loan that you swipe.*

Why Credit Cards Seem Easy — But Can Get Dangerous

What Feels Easy	What Actually Happens
"I'll just pay it later"	You forget, miss the deadline, and get charged interest
"I only owe $40 this month"	That's just the **minimum payment** — interest builds on the rest
"Everyone has a credit card"	Yes — and many people are in silent debt because of it
"I need it for emergencies"	If you rely on it too often, emergencies become expensive loans

Real-World Example: Meet Kai

What happened:
Kai got a credit card with a $1,000 limit. He used it for small things — takeout, gas, a few clothes — thinking he'd pay it off later. He paid the **minimum** ($25/month) for months.

What went wrong:
The interest added up. His balance grew to **$1,300** over time — without buying anything new. He felt stuck and frustrated.

What we learn:
Paying only the minimum doesn't make debt go away. It **stretches it out and costs you more.**

Key Terms You Must Know

Term	What It Means
Balance	The amount you owe right now
Credit Limit	The max you can borrow on your card
Minimum Payment	The smallest amount you *must* pay monthly
Interest Rate (APR)	The cost of borrowing if you don't pay the full balance
Due Date	The day your payment is due

📌 *If you ignore any of these, you could end up paying way more than expected.*

The Trap: Minimum Payments

Let's say you charge $500 and only pay the **minimum** of $25/month. If your interest rate is 20%, it could take **2+ years** to pay it off — and cost you over **$150 extra** in interest.

The card didn't cost $500 anymore. It cost **$650+** — for the same stuff.

📌 *Minimum payments keep you in debt. Paying in full gets you out.*

The Benefits (If Used Right)

Not all credit cards are bad. In fact, they can be helpful if you're smart:

- **Builds your credit score** (helps with renting, car loans, future mortgages)
- **Offers fraud protection** — better than a debit card
- **Rewards and points** — for things like groceries or travel
- **Useful in emergencies** — if you pay it off quickly

But all of these only work **if you pay your full balance on time every month**.

Tactical Best Practices

- ☑ Use your card for **small, planned purchases only**
- ☑ Set a reminder for the **due date** — never pay late
- ☑ Pay the **full balance** every month (not just the minimum)
- ☑ Only charge what you already have the money for
- ☑ Use one card to start — avoid juggling multiple accounts
- ☑ Set up **auto-pay** to avoid missed payments

Common Mistakes to Avoid

- Using credit for wants instead of needs
- Treating the credit limit like "extra cash"
- Ignoring interest rates — they grow fast
- Carrying a balance month after month
- Missing payments — it damages your credit score
- Getting multiple cards before you've mastered one

Checklist: Use Credit Cards Without the Stress

☑ Only use your card if you can pay it off this month
☑ Never spend more than 30% of your credit limit
☑ Always pay on or before the due date
☑ Check your statement weekly (many apps help you do this)
☑ Know your interest rate — and avoid letting it kick in
☑ Treat it like cash you already have, not future money

Conclusion

Credit cards are **tools** — not toys. They can help you build your financial future or quietly build debt you never meant to have.

Used wisely, they work for you. Used carelessly, they work *against* you.

The secret is simple: **Respect the card. Stick to your plan. Never borrow what you can't repay.**

AI Tips for Paying Debt Faster

Paying off debt can feel like climbing a hill — slow, tiring, and never-ending. But AI (Artificial Intelligence) can turn that steep climb into a **step-by-step staircase**, helping you make smarter moves, stay on track, and become debt-free sooner.

AI doesn't just track your debt — it gives you **real advice**, personalized plans, and automatic nudges that help you pay it down faster, without needing to be a financial expert.

Let's look at exactly how it works — and how to use it to your advantage.

How AI Helps You Pay Debt Faster

AI-powered apps and tools do things a regular budget can't. They can:

- Spot extra money in your account to put toward debt
- Help you choose the best repayment method (like avalanche vs. snowball)
- Send reminders so you never miss a payment
- Predict when you'll be debt-free — and how to get there faster
- Adjust your plan automatically when your income or spending changes

📌 *The result: faster progress with less effort and guesswork.*

Real-World Example: Meet Elena

What happened:
Elena had 3 credit cards with small balances and didn't know where to start. Her AI budgeting app analyzed her spending and suggested the **"snowball" method** — paying off the smallest balance first to build momentum.

It also:

- Found $30/week she could redirect toward her debt
- Automatically reminded her of upcoming payments
- Showed her a debt-free timeline — **4 months sooner** than she expected

What changed:
Elena stayed motivated, stayed consistent, and paid off her cards without burnout. The AI didn't just give her numbers — it gave her a plan.

Top AI-Powered Tools for Paying Off Debt

App	What It Helps With
Tally	Combines your credit cards and pays them off efficiently using AI
Cleo	Gives simple, direct advice on where to cut spending and boost debt payments
Undebt.it	Creates personalized debt repayment strategies with visual progress charts
YNAB (You Need a Budget)	Helps you budget around debt and allocate extra money where it counts
Monarch Money	Tracks debt balances, interest, and shows your payoff timeline in real time

📌 *These apps don't just track — they **guide.***

5 Smart AI Tips to Pay Off Debt Faster

✅ 1. Use AI to Find "Hidden" Money in Your Budget

Many budgeting apps will review your spending patterns and suggest where you can cut back:

- Unused subscriptions
- Eating out too often
- Overlapping expenses

That "found" money can go straight to your debt.

☑ 2. Let AI Suggest the Best Payoff Strategy

There are two main strategies:

- **Snowball:** Pay off the smallest debt first to gain momentum
- **Avalanche:** Pay off the debt with the highest interest first to save money

AI tools analyze your numbers and suggest the method that will work best **for your situation.**

☑ 3. Get Real-Time Reminders to Avoid Late Fees

Late payments = more debt and lower credit scores. AI apps remind you **before** it's due, so you never forget.

📌 *Some even send alerts when your bank account is too low to make a payment — helping you avoid overdrafts too.*

☑ 4. Use Round-Ups and Micro-Saving Toward Debt

Apps like **Qapital** and **Digit** let you round up purchases (like turning a $3.60 coffee into $4.00), and use the extra cents to make small debt payments.

📌 *It adds up over time — and you barely feel it.*

☑ 5. Track Your Progress Visually

AI tools show your progress in real time:

- How much interest you've avoided
- How far you've come
- How much time you've shaved off

Seeing progress keeps you motivated — and more likely to stick with your plan.

Tactical Best Practices

- **Choose one AI app to manage your debt plan** — don't bounce between too many tools
- **Use automatic payments** for your minimums, and manually add extra when you can
- **Set your app to show a "debt-free countdown"** — it helps with motivation
- **Focus on one card or loan at a time** — scatter-paying doesn't work as well
- **Let the AI adjust your plan** if your income changes (many apps do this)

Common Mistakes to Avoid

- Ignoring AI suggestions because they seem "too small" — $5/day adds up
- Stopping payments as soon as one card is paid off — roll it into the next one
- Missing payments because you rely on memory instead of reminders
- Trying to pay off everything at once without a strategy
- Not checking progress — it's the fuel that keeps you going

Checklist: Use AI to Crush Your Debt Faster

☑ Choose an AI-powered app that fits your style (simple or detailed)

☑ Link your accounts and debts so it can calculate accurately

☑ Let the app recommend a repayment strategy (snowball or avalanche)

☑ Set up reminders or auto-pay to avoid missing due dates

☑ Use extra money found by the app toward your top debt

☑ Celebrate small wins — like paying off your first card

Conclusion

AI doesn't replace your discipline — it strengthens it. By helping you plan, track, and stay on top of your debt, it turns a long, confusing journey into a clear, guided path.

And the best part? You don't have to figure it all out alone.

Let the tech do the heavy lifting — so you can focus on making progress, faster than you thought possible.

CHAPTER 8

Your Money Future

How Small Habits Make Big Change

When people think about getting better with money, they often imagine big moves: paying off a huge loan, saving thousands, or completely cutting out spending.

But here's the truth:

You don't need to be perfect. You need to be **consistent.**
And it's the **small habits**, repeated over time, that make the biggest difference.

Let's talk about how those tiny, everyday money choices can add up to real success — without overwhelm, pressure, or stress.

Why Small Habits Work Better Than Big Bursts

Trying to make a huge change all at once often leads to burnout. You might try a strict budget, cut out everything fun, and go all in… for a week. Then you fall off.

But when you build **small, easy habits** — things you can do without thinking — you create automatic progress.
Over time, those small wins **multiply**.

📌 *It's not about doing more — it's about doing a little, every day or week, on purpose.*

Real-World Example: Meet Jalen

What happened:
Jalen wanted to save $500, but every time he tried, he'd give up after 2 weeks. It felt impossible.

So he tried a new approach:

- Saved **$5 a day** using a round-up savings app
- Checked his spending every Sunday for 10 minutes
- Used AI to send him reminders when he was close to overspending

What changed:
After 3 months, Jalen had saved over **$460** — without making any huge sacrifices.
The small habits worked where big pressure failed.

Examples of Small Financial Habits That Actually Work

Habit	Time Needed	Long-Term Result
Save $1–$5/day into a separate account	1 minute	$30–$150/month saved
Check your bank app every Sunday	5–10 minutes/week	Stay aware and avoid overdrafts
Use cash or prepaid card for "fun" spending	Daily spending control	Stops impulse swipes
Log every purchase over $20	10 seconds per entry	Creates mindful spending
Set a reminder for bill due dates	1 time setup	Avoid late fees and credit damage
Skip one takeout meal per week	No effort needed	Save $40–$60/month
Use AI to suggest weekly debt payments	Passive	Pay off debt faster with less thinking

Why This Works: The Habit Loop

Every habit follows a simple loop:

1. **Cue** → You get a reminder or trigger (ex: phone buzzes)
2. **Action** → You do the habit (ex: check your budget)
3. **Reward** → You feel progress (ex: "I'm still on track!")

💡 *Repeat this loop enough, and the habit sticks. Then it runs on autopilot.*

AI Can Help Reinforce Good Habits

Modern money apps use AI to:

- Track your behavior
- Suggest tiny improvements
- Send reminders to keep you going
- Celebrate small wins to keep motivation high

Example:
Your app notices you've saved $20 two weeks in a row. It sends you a message:
"Nice job! At this rate, you'll hit your goal 1 week early."
That positive feedback builds confidence — and makes the habit feel worth it.

Tactical Best Practices

- **Pick 2–3 small habits to start** — not 10 at once
- **Use reminders** (calendar, app alerts, sticky notes)
- **Let AI tools automate part of the habit** (savings, check-ins, payments)
- **Track streaks** — how many days/weeks in a row you've followed through
- **Celebrate small wins** — they're not small when they add up

Common Mistakes to Avoid

- Trying to do everything all at once
- Quitting after one bad day — consistency matters more than perfection
- Not measuring progress (it's hard to stay motivated without visible wins)
- Comparing your pace to others — your money journey is yours
- Thinking small changes "don't matter" — they *always* do

Checklist: Build Small Habits That Stick

- ☑ Choose a habit that takes less than 10 minutes
- ☑ Tie it to something you already do (ex: check finances after your morning coffee)
- ☑ Use tools to remind or automate it
- ☑ Track how often you complete the habit (apps or paper)
- ☑ Celebrate every 7-day or monthly streak
- ☑ Adjust if it's too hard — simplify, don't quit

Conclusion

You don't need a raise, a loan, or a miracle to improve your finances. You just need a few small, smart habits — repeated over time.

$1 saved, $1 less spent, one good decision per day. That's how real financial change begins. It doesn't happen overnight — but it absolutely happens.

Start small. Stay steady. And trust the process.

Planning for Big Dreams (Travel, Home, Business)

Everyone has a dream.
It might be to visit another country, own a cozy apartment, or turn a creative idea into a real business.

But here's the truth most people miss:

Big dreams don't happen by accident. They happen through planning, patience, and small steps — starting now.

Even if you're just getting started with money, you don't need to wait until "someday." You can begin laying the foundation today, even with just a few dollars at a time.

Let's talk about how to plan for the *big stuff* — using clear steps, smart habits, and tools that keep you moving forward.

Why Big Dreams Matter

A big dream isn't just something "nice to have." It gives you a reason to:

- Stay focused with your money
- Build better habits
- Save more with purpose
- Say no to things that don't serve you

📌 *When you have a big goal, your everyday choices start working for your future — not just for the moment.*

Three Popular Big Dreams (and How to Plan for Them)

Let's walk through **how to plan** for three common dreams: **Travel**, **Home**, and **Starting a Business** — using real numbers and beginner-friendly strategies.

✈️ Dream #1: Travel (Local or International)

Travel can be expensive, but with a plan, it becomes possible — even fun.

Example Goal: Trip to New York next summer — $1,200 total
Includes: Flight, 3 nights hotel, food, transit, activities

Step-by-step plan:

- Timeline: 10 months
- $1,200 ÷ 10 = **$120/month or $30/week**
- Use a **separate savings account** or travel app to track it
- Use AI tools to:
  - Set savings reminders
  - Find cheaper travel dates or accommodations
  - Predict how early you'll hit your goal if you save extra

♀ Tip: Use round-up apps (like Qapital) to save small amounts daily — you won't even notice it.

⌂ Dream #2: Buying a Home (Or First Apartment)

Even if you're years away, it's smart to start saving now. First homes or apartments require:

- **Down payment or deposit**
- First month's rent + damage deposit
- Moving costs
- Furniture and basics

Starter Goal Example:
Save $3,000 in 18 months = about **$167/month**

How to get there:

- Set a goal in your banking or budgeting app
- Let AI analyze your current expenses and suggest what you can safely put aside
- Use "goal buckets" (many apps offer this) to keep it separate from everyday money

♀ Tip: Even saving just $10–$20/week builds the habit — and proves to yourself that the dream is real.

Dream #3: Starting a Small Business or Side Hustle

Starting a business doesn't require thousands. Many creative side hustles (photography, tutoring, art, digital sales) can begin with a few hundred dollars.

Example Goal: $1,000 to launch a small clothing brand
Covers: Domain, logo design, starter inventory, website

Planning Strategy:

- Break it down: $1,000 in 6 months = **$167/month**
- Use AI to:
  - Recommend where to cut small expenses to save faster
  - Track your progress automatically
  - Give you weekly reminders to stay focused
- Consider using **spending limit cards** (like prepaid or debit cards) to keep launch costs on track

💡 *Tip: Dream big, start small. The goal isn't perfection — it's* **progress.**

Real-World Example: Meet Layla

What happened:
Layla wanted to visit Japan in 2 years — a $3,000 trip. She had never saved that much before.

What she did:

- Set a weekly savings target of $30
- Used an AI savings app to automate transfers
- Got monthly updates on her progress
- Used a cashback rewards card for everyday purchases and put the rewards into her trip fund

The result:
She booked her flight 2 months early — and had money left over for souvenirs.

Tactical Best Practices for Big Goals

- **Name your goal clearly** — "Paris 2026" or "First Business Fund"
- **Break big goals into monthly or weekly chunks**
- **Use AI budgeting apps** to:
  - Recommend how much you can save
  - Show timelines and progress
  - Adjust based on income changes
- **Track visually** — goal bars, jars, or printables keep it real
- **Review every month** — small updates = long-term success

Common Mistakes to Avoid

- Setting goals with no clear dollar amount or timeline
- Saving into the same account you spend from
- Thinking "I'll start when I earn more" — start with what you have
- Giving up after missing one savings week — adjust, don't quit
- Forgetting to track progress — you can't celebrate what you don't see

Checklist: Build a Plan for Your Big Dream

- [x] Choose a goal: travel, home, business — something *real* to you
- [x] Find out what it will actually cost
- [x] Pick a realistic deadline
- [x] Divide the total into weekly or monthly saving chunks
- [x] Use an AI-powered app to track it automatically
- [x] Review your progress once a month and adjust if needed
- [x] Keep a visual reminder (phone background, wall chart, etc.)

Conclusion

Big dreams aren't just for "someday." With a simple plan, smart tools, and small consistent steps, you can turn **someday** into **real soon.**

You don't need to wait. You just need to start. Your future is something you build — one choice, one week, one saved dollar at a time.

Staying Safe from Scams

Scams are everywhere — in your inbox, text messages, social media, and even phone calls. And if you're just starting to manage money, you're a **prime target**.

Why? Because scammers love to trick people who are new to budgeting, banking, or using apps. But don't worry — with a few simple rules, you can protect yourself and your money.

A scam is anytime someone lies to get your money or personal information.
If something feels rushed, secretive, or "too good to be true," it probably is.

Let's break down how to spot a scam, what to do if you see one, and how to stay safe without getting paranoid.

What Scammers Want

Scammers are after two things:

1. **Your money**
2. **Your personal information** (so they can steal your money later)

They might pretend to be:

- Your bank
- A delivery company
- A government agency
- A job recruiter
- A tech support agent
- Even someone you know (via hacked accounts)

📌 *They want you to trust them quickly — and act fast before you stop and think.*

Common Scams to Watch Out For

Scam Type	How It Works	Red Flags
Phishing Emails or Texts	Fake messages pretending to be your bank, Netflix, Amazon, etc.	"Click this link now" or "Your account is locked"
Fake Job Offers	You're hired instantly, then asked for personal info or to pay upfront	No interview, vague job details
Online Marketplace Scams	Someone overpays you and asks for a refund — then the original money disappears	"I accidentally sent you too much, send some back"
Romance Scams	Fake relationships that lead to money requests	Love talk turns into "Can you help me with something?"
Tech Support Scams	Pop-ups say your device has a virus — you're told to download "fixes" or give access	"Call this number immediately" or "You've been hacked"
Fake Prize or Lottery Scams	"You've won!" but you need to pay a fee to claim the prize	You never entered a contest, but somehow won it

Real-World Example: Meet Alex

What happened:
Alex got a text that looked like it was from his bank: "Fraud alert! Click here to confirm your identity."

He clicked the link and entered his account info.

What went wrong:
The site was fake. His bank account was emptied within hours.

What we learn:
Banks will never ask you to click a link and enter your full login details. If it feels urgent and scary, it's often a scam.

How to Stay Safe: 5 Simple Rules

✅ **1. Never Share Personal Info Over Messages**

- No bank, government office, or legit company will ask for your:
    - PIN
    - Full password
    - Social Security Number (unless you're applying for something official)
    - Banking info by text or DM

📌 *If someone asks — it's a red flag.*

✅ 2. Don't Click Suspicious Links

- Hover over a link (or long-press on mobile) to see where it leads.
- If it looks weird, misspelled, or unfamiliar — **don't click.**

Example:

- **Legit:** `bankofamerica.com`
- **Scam:** `bank-of-america-login-help.co`

📌 *One wrong click can infect your device or steal your info.*

✅ 3. Check First, Act Later

If something feels off:

- Call the real company using a **number from their website** — not the one in the message
- Ask a trusted friend or adult for a second opinion
- Google the message or phone number with the word **"scam"** — you might find warnings

📌 *Scammers want you to panic and act fast. Slow down, and they lose.*

✅ 4. Use Two-Factor Authentication (2FA)

Turn on 2FA for all important accounts (banking, email, social media).
This means even if someone gets your password, they still need a code from your phone to log in.

📌 *It adds one extra step — but it blocks a lot of attacks.*

☑ 5. Use AI Security Tools and Scam Alerts

Some budgeting apps and banks now use AI to detect suspicious activity, like:

- Sudden transfers to unknown accounts
- Logins from strange locations
- Unusual purchase patterns

They'll alert you if something doesn't match your normal behavior.

📌 *Let the tech work for you. Turn on all available alerts.*

Common Mistakes to Avoid

- Thinking "It could never happen to me"
- Rushing to click a link before thinking
- Ignoring weird spelling or urgent messages
- Sending money to "friends" you've only met online
- Not checking official sources before acting

Checklist: Stay Scam-Safe

☑ Never share private info over text, DM, or email
☑ Don't click links you don't trust — check first
☑ Use strong passwords and 2FA
☑ Turn on fraud alerts in your banking app
☑ Talk to someone you trust if anything feels weird
☑ When in doubt, **delete or ignore** the message

Conclusion
Scams don't just target "old people" or "rich people." They target *everyone* — especially beginners who are still learning.

But now you know the signs. And if you stay alert, take your time, and use the right tools, you can protect your money and your future.

AI as Your Money Helper for Life

You've come a long way. You've learned what money in vs. money out really means. You've built your first budget, started saving, understood debt, spotted scams, and discovered how small habits lead to big results.

Now it's time to look ahead — because this isn't the end of your journey. It's the beginning of a lifetime of **smart, confident money decisions.**
And the good news is:

You don't have to do it all on your own.
AI can be your lifelong money helper — quietly guiding, tracking, and protecting your financial future.

Let's close this chapter with a look at how to keep growing, keep learning, and keep using AI as a powerful partner in your money life.

What "AI as a Money Helper" Really Means

AI (artificial intelligence) sounds like a big, technical word. But in your everyday life, it's simply:

- An app that watches your spending and helps you stay on track
- A chatbot that gives advice without judgment
- A tool that automates your savings and payments
- A system that notices patterns you'd miss
- A coach that keeps showing up, even when you're tired

📌 *It's not about robots. It's about getting smart help, when you need it, so you don't fall behind.*

What AI Will Keep Doing for You (Long-Term)

As your life changes — maybe you get your first job, move to a new place, start a family, or launch a business — your money needs will grow too.

AI tools will be right there with you, helping you:

Life Stage	How AI Helps
First Job	Track your new income, build your first serious budget
Living on Your Own	Monitor rent, bills, and groceries — and alert you when you're overspending
Paying Off Debt	Recommend faster payoff strategies and automate payments
Saving for Big Goals	Visualize your timeline and automatically adjust your plan
Running a Business	Manage income vs. expenses, taxes, and invoices with smart dashboards
Planning for Retirement	Help you invest, automate contributions, and reduce risk over time

💡 *AI adapts to your life — and grows with you.*

Real-World Example: Meet Dani

What happened:
Dani started with a $20/week savings goal using an AI budgeting app. Over 3 years, her income grew, her life changed — and so did her goals.

Her app kept up. It helped her:

- Track her side hustle income
- Automate credit card payments
- Save for a car
- Avoid late fees
- Get weekly progress reports

Now she's preparing to buy her first home — and the same AI tools are guiding her every step of the way.

What we learn:
You don't need to be an expert. You just need to start — and keep going.

Tactical Best Practices for Using AI Long-Term

- **Review your money app weekly** — even for 5 minutes
- **Update your goals every 6 months** — AI can help adjust your plan
- **Keep alerts turned on** — they're your early-warning system
- **Let AI automate things you forget** — transfers, bills, reminders
- **Use visual goal tracking** to stay motivated
- **Check your trends every month** — are you saving more? Spending less?

Common Mistakes to Avoid (Even Later On)

- Thinking you've "learned enough" and ignoring your money again
- Turning off reminders because "you're good now"
- Getting overwhelmed by too many tools — keep it simple
- Comparing your financial progress to others
- Forgetting to dream bigger — your goals will grow, and AI can help them grow with you

Final Checklist: Keep AI as Your Lifelong Money Partner

☑ Use one core budgeting app that tracks income, expenses, and savings

☑ Automate your savings and debt payments

☑ Let AI recommend changes as your life evolves

☑ Stay consistent with weekly check-ins

☑ Adjust your goals as your income, needs, or dreams change

☑ Trust your tools — but always stay informed

☑ Keep learning — curiosity is your greatest money skill

Conclusion: You're in Control Now

You don't need to be rich to feel confident about money. You don't need to be perfect, or know everything, or "have it all figured out."

You just need to:

- Know what's coming in
- Know what's going out
- Spend on purpose
- Save with direction
- Use smart tools to stay on track

And now — **you do**.

This book gave you the foundations:

☑ A clear budget

☑ A savings plan

☑ Awareness of scams and debt

☑ Big goals broken into small steps

☑ The power of habits

☑ And the smart support of AI every step of the way

You're not starting from scratch anymore. You're starting **from strength.**

Next Steps for Your Money Journey

- **Choose one AI-powered app** today and set up your weekly budget check-in
- **Write down one dream** (travel, home, business) and start saving — even if it's $1/week
- **Turn on alerts and security features** on your bank and budgeting apps
- **Review your progress monthly** and adjust as needed
- **Keep learning** — you've built the habit, now grow it

This isn't goodbye — it's your new beginning.
You've got the tools, the knowledge, and the power.

And now, you've got **AI as your money helper for life.**

Glossary of Money Terms (Simple Definitions)

Here's a quick and easy glossary of the key money words used in this book. These definitions are written in simple, beginner-friendly language — no complicated jargon or confusing financial talk.

Use this as a go-to reference any time you're unsure about a term.

A–C

AI (Artificial Intelligence)
Smart technology that can help you manage money, track spending, and make financial decisions automatically.

Allowance
Money you might receive regularly from parents or guardians, often for doing chores or meeting expectations.

Auto-Save
When an app or bank automatically moves money into your savings account — no need to do it yourself each time.

Balance (Bank Account)
The total amount of money you currently have in your bank account.

Balance (Credit Card)
The amount of money you owe on your credit card after making purchases.

Bill
A payment you need to make regularly (like rent, phone, or streaming service).

Budget
A simple plan for how you'll use your money — what's coming in, what's going out, and what's saved.

Buy Now, Pay Later (BNPL)
A way to buy something now and pay for it in small amounts over time (often used online). Can lead to debt if not managed well.

Credit
Money you borrow and promise to pay back later (usually through a credit card or loan).

Credit Card
A card that lets you borrow money from a bank or lender to make purchases. You must pay it back — often with interest.

Credit Limit
The maximum amount you're allowed to borrow on a credit card.

Credit Score
A number (usually between 300–850) that shows how good you are at managing debt. Higher is better. It affects your ability to borrow money in the future.

D–F

Debt
Money you owe to someone else, like a bank, lender, or even a friend. Debt must be paid back — usually with extra fees or interest.

Deposit (Bank)
Money you put into a bank account.

Emergency Fund
Money saved in case something unexpected happens, like losing a job or needing to fix something important.

Expense
Anything you spend money on — like food, bills, clothes, or subscriptions.

Fraud Alert
A warning from your bank or app when something suspicious happens with your account.

Financial Goal
A money target you want to reach — like saving for a trip, paying off debt, or buying a laptop.

G–M

Good Debt
Debt that helps you grow, like student loans or a small business loan — as long as you can manage it.

Income
Money you earn or receive — from a job, allowance, gift, or business.

Interest (on Debt)
Extra money you must pay when you borrow money. It's how lenders make money.

Investment
Using money to try to grow your money — like buying stocks or putting money into a retirement fund. (Not covered deeply in this book.)

Loan
Money someone gives you to use now, with the agreement that you'll pay it back over time.

Minimum Payment
The smallest amount you must pay on a loan or credit card each month to stay in good standing.

Mobile Banking App
An app that lets you manage your money on your phone — check your balance, send payments, track spending.

N–S

Needs
Essential things you must have to live — like food, rent, medicine, transportation.

Overspending
Spending more money than you planned — or more than you have.

Principal (Loan)
The original amount of money you borrowed — not including interest.

Round-Up Saving
A feature where purchases are rounded up to the next dollar, and the extra cents go into your savings.

Saving
Setting aside part of your money for later use — either short-term (for fun or emergencies) or long-term (like a home or business).

Scam
A trick where someone tries to steal your money or personal information by lying or pretending to be someone else.

Snowball Method
A way to pay off debt by starting with the smallest balance first, to build momentum.

Spending Habit
Your pattern of how, where, and when you spend money — good or bad.

Subscription
A regular payment for something like a streaming service, app, or product.

T–Z

Transfer
Moving money from one account to another.

Two-Factor Authentication (2FA)
An extra security step when logging into accounts — usually a password plus a code sent to your phone.

Wants
Things you enjoy but don't *need* to survive — like takeout, new clothes, or a game.

Weekly Money Routine
A short check-in with your budget and spending once a week to stay on track.

Final Tip:
Whenever you see a money term you don't understand, ask yourself:

- Is this about money coming in?
- Money going out?
- Borrowing or saving?
- Planning or reacting?

Keeping it simple is always the smartest way to learn.
You've got this — and now, you've got the words to match.

Thank You — And One Small Favor!

Thank you so much for reading this book. We hope it gave you the clarity, confidence, and practical tools you needed to take control of your money — one small step at a time.

If this book helped you, taught you something new, or simply made budgeting feel less overwhelming, we'd be incredibly grateful if you took a moment to leave a review on Amazon.

Your review doesn't need to be long — even a few honest words makes a huge difference. It helps other readers discover the book, and it helps us continue creating content that truly serves real people like you.

Your voice matters. Your feedback matters. And your review? It might just be the reason someone else finally starts their own money journey.

Please leave a review on Amazon — it only takes a minute, but it means the world.

Thank you again — and here's to a future where you feel calm, confident, and in control of your finances.

Thanks for being part of this journey,
Eric LeBouthillier
Author